W9-AZT-744

COVENANT • BIBLE • STUDIES

A Spirituality of Compassion
Studies in Luke

Harriet Finney and
Suzanne DeMoss Martin

faithQuest® ✦ Brethren Press®

Library of Congress Catalog Card Number: 96-84192

Contents

Foreword

The Covenant Bible Study Series was first developed for a denominational program in the Church of the Brethren and the Christian Church (Disciples of Christ). This program, called People of the Covenant, was founded on the concept of relational Bible study and has been adopted by several other denominations and small groups who want to study the Bible in a community rather than alone.

Relational Bible study is marked by certain characteristics, some of which differ from other types of Bible study. For one, it is intended for small groups of people who can meet face-to-face on a regular basis and share frankly with an intimate group.

It is important to remember that relational Bible study is anchored in covenantal history. God covenanted with people in Old Testament history, established a new covenant in Jesus Christ, and covenants with the church today.

Relational Bible study takes seriously a corporate faith. As each person contributes to study, prayer, and work, the group becomes the real body of Christ. Each one's contribution is needed and important. "For just as the body is one and has many members, and all the members of the body, though many, are one body, so it is with Christ. . . . Now you are the body of Christ and individually members of it" (1 Cor. 12:12,17).

Relational Bible study helps both individuals and the group to claim the promise of the Spirit and the working of the Spirit. As one person testified, "In our commitment to one another and in our sharing, something happened. . . . We were woven together in love by the master Weaver. It is something that can happen only when two or three or seven are gathered in God's name, and we know the promise of God's presence in our lives."

The symbol of these covenant Bible study groups is the burlap cross. The interwoven threads, the uniqueness of each strand, the unrefined fabric, and the rough texture characterize covenant groups. The people in the groups are unique but interrelated; they are imperfect and unpolished, but loving and supportive.

The shape that these divergent threads create is the cross, the symbol for all Christians of the resurrection and presence with us of Christ our Savior. Like the burlap cross, we are brought together, simple and ordinary, to be sent out again in all directions to be in the world.

For people who choose to use this study in a small group, the following guidelines will help create an atmosphere in which support will grow and faith will deepen.

1. As a small group of learners, we gather around God's word to discern its meaning for today.
2. The words, stories, and admonitions we find in scripture come alive for today, challenging and renewing us.
3. All people are learners and all are leaders.
4. Each person will contribute to the study, sharing the meaning found in the scripture and helping to bring meaning to others.
5. We recognize each other's vulnerability as we share out of our own experience, and in sharing we learn to trust others and to be trustworthy.

Additional suggestions for study and group-building are provided in the "Sharing and Prayer" section. They are intended for use in the hour preceding the Bible study to foster intimacy in the covenant group and relate personal sharing to the Bible study topic.

Welcome to this study. As you search the scriptures, may you also search yourself. May God's voice and guidance and the love and encouragement of brothers and sisters in Christ challenge you to live more fully the abundant life God promises.

Preface

One of my earliest "mountaintop experiences" came the summer I was ten years old—my first week at Camp Bethel in southern Virginia. Living in log cabins, talking and singing and studying, climbing up the Blue Ridge mountains to Horseshoe Bend, getting up early for morning watch around the spring, trudging over to Vesper Hill for evening prayers—so many things made this a "mountaintop" for me. I did not want to go home at the end of the week!

Mountaintop experiences continued through my teen years at youth camps, district and regional roundtables, national youth conferences—places where I met God and myself in deeper ways, times when I decided to follow Jesus.

Adults know about mountaintop experiences too. A two-week visit with Nigerian brothers and sisters became such a time for me. We worshiped and ate together; we sang and prayed together. I soaked up loving hospitality in village homes, in rural and city churches. My own faith deepened as I experienced my new friends' depth of devotion to Christ and his church. And again, just as when I was ten years old, I found it difficult to come down from that mountaintop.

Peter, James, and John with Jesus on the Mount of Transfiguration also found it difficult to leave a spiritual high and come down to the frustrations, the demands, the fragmentation of valley living. And yet Jesus challenged them to find the important connection between the faith of the mountaintop and life lived in the valley.

A Spirituality of Compassion calls us to hear that same challenge. How do we bring our mountaintops and our valleys together? What transformation is needed to integrate our spirit-lives and our action-lives? What unites the inner aspects and the outer aspects of our spirituality?

A definition of spirituality that speaks to me is this: "True spirituality is where compassion and contemplation meet." Compassion, to me, means moving deeply into the lives of others, meeting them at their points of need, being met at my own points of need. Contemplation, to me, means moving deeply into relationship with God, meeting God and being met by God.

We see this rhythm of compassion and contemplation in Jesus' life. He left the Mount of Transfiguration and healed a boy with a convulsive spirit. He moved often from quiet prayer and solitary times with God into people's lives, healing, teaching, preaching. He connected deep caring for others with intentional care for himself—an integrated life. What a model of the spirituality of compassion! What a model for us! This study, *A Spirituality of Compassion,* will call us to new understandings and expressions of spirituality—a spirituality that reaches deeply into the spirit, a spirituality that reaches widely out to others. A spirituality in which compassion and contemplation meet.

—June Adams Gibble, Coordinator
People of the Covenant

Recommended Resources:

Bonhoeffer, Dietrich. *The Cost of Discipleship.* New York: Macmillan, 1961.

Craddock, Fred B. *Luke* (Interpretation Series). Louisville, Ky.: Westminster John Knox, 1990.

Gabriele, Edward F. *Act Justly, Love Tenderly, Walk Humbly.* Winona, Minn.: St Mary's Press, 1995.

McGinnis, James. *Journey Into Compassion.* Bloomington, Ind.: Meyer-Stone, 1989.

Nouwen, Henri. *Reaching Out.* Garden City, N.Y.: Doubleday, 1975.

Nouwen, Henri. *The Wounded Healer.* Garden City, N.Y.: Image Books, 1972.

Thomas, Leo. *The Healing Team: A Practical Guide for Effective Ministry.* New York: Paulist Press, 1987.

1

You Can't Force the Heart
Luke 4:1-30

Having been baptized and tempted in the wilderness, Jesus taught in Nazareth's synagogue that his ministry of compassion would extend to all people. For this he was rejected even by those in his hometown. We should not be surprised at the challenge that comes with reaching out. We are called to act with compassion, but it is never easy or painless, and it cannot be forced.

Personal Preparation

1. Read Luke 4:1-30. List some of the experiences and "qualifications" that prepared Jesus for his ministry of compassion. Place a star by those that seem necessary for anyone who wants to reach out to others in need.

2. Spend some time considering what inspires and moves you to acts of compassion. How would you describe the relationship between your desire to be compassionate and the health of your devotional life?

3. Identify a time in your past when you made a commitment before everything about the situation was clear. Was that an easy step to take? What challenges did you face?

Understanding

"I had gone to a nursing home with a youth group from my church," wrote Sue Monk Kidd in a *Weavings* article. "Frankly, I was there under duress. My mother had not heard my pleas that I be spared the unjust sentence of visiting a nursing home when my friends were enjoying the last day of summer vacation at the city swimming pool.

Smarting from the inequity, I stood before this ancient-looking woman, holding a bouquet of crepe-paper flowers. Everything about her saddened me—the worn-down face, the lopsided grin, the tendrils of gray hair protruding from a crocheted lavender cap. I thrust the bouquet at her. She looked at me, a look that pierced me to the marrow of my twelve-year-old bones. Then she spoke the words I have not forgotten for nearly thirty years. 'You didn't want to come, did you, child?'

"The words stunned me. They were too painful, too powerful, too naked in their honesty. 'Oh yes, I wanted to come,' I protested. A smile lifted one side of her mouth. 'It's okay,' she said. 'You can't force the heart.'

"I tried to forget her. For awhile I hated her for the rebuke. Then I passed it off as the harmless twittering of an old woman. Years later though, as I began to follow the labyrinth of my spiritual journey, I discovered the truth in her words."

Sue points to something we may know intuitively but may never consciously admit. We cannot merely make up our minds to be compassionate. Rather, we choose a way of living in fellowship with God, a spiritual journey that gradually changes the heart into a locus of mercy. For, as Sue wrote, "Compassion is the very life of God within us."

Compassion was a primary theme for Luke. As a physician he clearly cared about people, having devoted his life to healing their hurts and meeting their physical needs. And Luke saw numerous spiritual needs in the early church, as well. One of them was the lack of an orderly, historical account of Jesus' life and teachings (see Luke 1:1-4). Luke also addressed another pressing concern: the delay in Christ's promised second coming. The earliest Christians expected the Lord to return in their own generation. When that did not happen, they had to learn to wait, to live together in community, to persevere in a world hostile to the church. Emphasizing the significance of the "present time," Luke focused on Jesus' concern for the poor, the socially outcast, the gentiles, and women.

All of these concerns flowed from Jesus' life of prayer and the activity of the Holy Spirit in him. As we study Luke's Gospel, then, let us try to discover how Jesus' deepening spirituality points the way for our own transformation into a compassionate people.

A Compassionate Journey

Jesus was on a journey, a journey of compassion that would eventually lead to his Passion. He himself chose this journey. It included temptation and severe testing, yet it was also a journey of acclaim to which people responded, a journey of healing that crossed others' paths with physical wholeness and spiritual renewal.

As he began his trek into the wilderness, Jesus struggled to understand God's intention for his ministry. The temptations to self-promotion were great. Three times the devil tried to coerce Jesus into abusing his power to do popular ministry. Turning stones into bread would have brought him the acclaim of hungry people. Demonstrating authority over the world's kingdoms might have led him to end all political oppression before the fullness of time. And proving himself divine with a spectacular miracle would surely have promoted church growth! Yet God was not calling Jesus to *popular* ministry, but to a ministry of compassion. No doubt Jesus was tempted, as we are, to do only the things we do well and for which we receive applause. True compassion, however, literally means "with" (com) "suffering" (passion)—suffering with others who are hurting. That will not be always popular, pleasant, or personally rewarding.

The ministry of Jesus flowed out of his understanding of the Jewish scriptures and his personal response to God's call. He grew up immersed in the scriptures and the religious tradition in his home, synagogue schools, and Sabbath worship. Then his baptism and his filling with the Holy Spirit, along with his struggle in the wilderness, enabled him to return to Galilee as an adult to worship. He was a hometown boy reading in public the familiar words of the prophet Isaiah, "The Spirit of the LORD is upon me, because he has anointed me to bring good news to the poor. He has sent me to proclaim release to the captives and recovery of sight to the blind, to let the oppressed go free, to proclaim the year of the LORD's favor" (Luke 4:18-19; Isa. 61:1-2). At first, the people liked Jesus' message because they assumed he spoke directly of them. They envisioned their lives becoming full, meaningful, and free from oppression. So they "spoke well of him" and his gracious words (4:22).

Then, in verse 23, we see the mood beginning to change. Jesus stopped short of reading a crucial phrase in the Isaiah passage about the destruction of enemies. Perhaps this brought the problem to a head, for some of the people from Jesus' hometown had already begun to question his ministry to others beyond Nazareth, especially to non-Jews. The people grew angry.

An Inclusive Healing

When confronted with difficult truths about themselves, people do tend to become angry. Nothing makes me angrier than when my husband reminds me of one of my faults, usually something I have already recognized but have done little to remedy. So we can understand the situation in the synagogue at Nazareth. The people there knew the scriptures. They no doubt knew, at least implicitly, that God's compassion and healing was inclusive, extending to all people. Such was the case with the widow of Zarephath in Sidon and the leper, Naaman the Syrian, to whom Jesus referred. Had Jesus' hearers found it more comfortable to compartmentalize and narrow the sphere of their own compassionate actions, would they have preferred that God follow their lead?

It is easier for any of us to bestow compassion only on those we choose for that blessing. But this was not the way of Jesus. When he reminded the people of God's much wider mercies, he was driven away (verses 29-30). Jesus' acceptance of his mission of compassion for all people led to his own rejection.

Etty Hillesum was a young woman living in Amsterdam during World War II. She was an intellectual woman of means and comfort, having friends in high and powerful places. Although she was born a Jew, she did not have a strong faith in God or much concern for others. As life became more difficult in Amsterdam, however, she experienced amazing spiritual growth. This new life of the spirit increased her joy and trust in God. And it eventually compelled her to make a tough decision: she would go with her family and friends as they were taken to the concentration camp at Westerbork. At the risk of her own life, she determined to bring light into the lives of starving, dying prisoners—people she once had little reason to include in her plans.

A decision for compassion worked a radical change in Etty's inner being. Read the last words she wrote in her diary before dying at Auschwitz on November 30, 1943: "We should be willing to act as a balm for *all* wounds." Compassion under the conditions Etty experienced could only come from a deep and abiding walk with God. Out of such fellowship she could write, "Once you have begun to walk with God, you need only keep walking with him and all of life becomes one long stroll."

A Daily Calling

That life-long "stroll" is a daily walk requiring constant growth in understanding and wisdom, for sometimes we become confused about what it actually means to extend true compassion. Consider the case of Tim, thirty-five years old and homeless. Far from his hometown and long out of work, he often sneaked into a cold attic above a garage for a few hours' sleep after a hard day on the streets of Chicago. Although Tim was an intelligent and capable person, he seemed incapable of holding a job for more than a week or two at a time. Joe, a local pastor, wanted to help Tim get his life together and invited him to live in the parsonage for several months. He provided a home, assistance in getting and keeping a job, and even arranged for counseling. However, it seemed that the more help Jim received, the more he needed. After Jim was back on the streets, still receiving encouragement from Joe, he finally got a job and was able to rent a small room.

In light of Tim's case, I am reminded once again of the practicality of compassion's definition: that it is suffering "with" not "for" someone else. Why? Because in trying to assist a newly hatched butterfly I may prevent it from developing its wings. If I allow a butterfly to struggle to fly, its wings can grow strong. In pushing the baby bird out of the nest the mother builds life-preserving self-sufficiency. I sometimes respond to the difficulties of others by rushing in to rescue them. It feels good to help, yet the most compassionate act may be to allow that dear person to struggle to reach a stage of growth I could never provide as a gift.

How do you and I prepare for living this life of true compassion? How can we learn to accept our own mission of compassion as Jesus did? It will not be easy. Suffering with others can bring much pain into our lives. That is the risk we must take. We may need and want to fix things immediately, but we may not be able to do so. We are called to remain with those who suffer, just as the God of Hosea, in the Old Testament, suffered with the Israelites. Graciously, God allowed them to make mistakes, to break relationships, to experience the devastation of foolish choices.

The example of Jesus points us to the first steps in our journey of compassion. In the Gospel of Luke we find Jesus' many acts of mercy set firmly in the context of his deep faith in God and in his belief that God wills the good of all creation. Luke also tells us that Jesus prayed frequently and that he counseled the disciples to talk with God, too, and not to lose heart. All of this added up to a daily calling, a close walk with God in intimate fellowship. Out of that daily walk compassion flowed.

So we can see that Jesus' compassion grew out of his life of faith and prayer as he committed himself to follow his Father's will. That is the key for us. We, too, need a *spirituality* of compassion, a transformation of mind and heart that begins with an open-souled acknowledgment before the Lord that we, as well, long to be "filled with the power of the

Spirit" (4:14). But we cannot wait to commit ourselves to compassion until we have perfected our life of faith. As writer Peter J. Henriot said, "Commitment is prior to intimacy. One must make an option, take a stand, before everything is clear." If compassion grows out of our life with Christ, then—in delightful paradox—our relationship with him is strengthened by every attempt at compassionate living.

Discussion and Action

1. Refer to number 1 in this chapter's Personal Preparation and talk about the experiences and qualifications that helped prepare Jesus for his ministry of compassion. If "being filled with the Spirit" (4:1,14,18) is crucial, what does that mean for people in your group?

2. Have you ever had an experience like Sue Monk Kidd's? With which person in her story do you most identify? Why?

3. What would you say is the basic meaning of the statement, "You can't force the heart"? When have you seen this principle at work in your own life?

4. When have you been the *recipient* of Christian compassion? What did it mean for you? Did you perceive and feel it as compassion at the time? Explain.

5. When we see someone suffering we often respond by feeling pain for that person. In practical terms, what does it mean to suffer "with" but not "for"? Can you offer an example from your own experience or observation?

6. Spend some time considering these excerpts from a denominational report about a sister-church relationship:

In 1995, the Bella Vista Church (in a predominantly Hispanic Los Angeles community) partnered with the Buena Vista Church (in a mostly white community in the Shenandoah Valley of Virginia), creating a project entitled *'Compañeros en Ministerio.'* The two congregations seek to answer the 'Macedonian call' as they develop shared ministries. Buena Vista has assisted Bella Vista with repairs to the church and has helped with its street ministry; Bella Vista will support Buena Vista in expanding its prison ministry as well as guiding the Virginia church as it begins cross-cultural outreach within its community.

In the coming weeks, you will be invited to explore the idea of sister-church partnerships. Developing such a relationship is a process that will take much longer than ten weeks, but it can begin with creative thinking, prayer, and information gathering. Some weeks you will discuss an aspect of such a ministry to familiarize yourselves with how it works (see explanations in the General Resources at the back of this book). Some groups will follow up with specific actions. Others will benefit just by thinking about and discussing ideas, perhaps inviting other church members to participate. In any case, ask the Holy Spirit to guide you. For now, share initial responses to the concept of sister-church relationships.

2

Being and Doing . . . in Balance
Luke 4:31-44

Jesus filled his days to the brim. From daybreak to sunset he went about teaching and healing in Galilee. But he also found time to be alone. For him, prayer was a critical component of a balanced commitment: the balance between being and doing.

Personal Preparation

1. Read Luke 4:31-44. From these verses, how would you describe a day in the life of Jesus? How did his activities help him fulfill his overall mission? Now think about what your "typical" day is like. In what ways do your daily activities move you to fulfill your basic purpose in life?

2. Spend a few moments thinking about your community. What situations in your community call for a compassionate response from believers? Which could require you, personally, to take action on behalf of others? What kinds of action come to mind?

3. Henri Nouwen said, "Waste a little time with God." How could you do that in the days preceding your group meeting? Make some plans for a few minutes of "holy wastefulness" this week.

Understanding

Remember riding the playground seesaw as a child? If your partner was a bit heavier than you, you were in for a wild ride! On the other hand, if you had the weight advantage, you could control the destiny of your unfortunate playmate, perhaps making her hang up in the air, begging for mercy.

When I consider Jesus' life of prayer and service, I sometimes think of that old seesaw on my elementary school playground. I envision the two children on each end being about the same size and therefore enjoying a perfectly balanced experience. Of course, most of the time seesaws do not stay perfectly balanced for very long. They continue to teeter up and down. Perhaps that imbalance is a more accurate portrayal of our spiritual lives.

A Balanced Commitment

Sometimes we are more comfortable on one end of the seesaw than the other. We may spend a great deal of time in Bible study, prayer, or worship. We may even attend a workshop or a concert to enhance our spiritual lives, but there is little evidence of action growing out of our Christian commitment. Or we may spend so much time enriching our spiritual lives that we become turned in on ourselves and forget the needs of others.

On the other hand, we may be "doing" for others constantly. We might participate in a CROP walk, visit in a nursing home, or regularly volunteer at a food pantry, yet spend very little time in prayer, meditation, and Bible study. It is even possible to become so service oriented that we almost forget that it is in Christ's name that we serve.

Both prayer and acts of compassion are essential if we are to follow in the footsteps of Jesus. Private devotion and public doing must be integrated, because neither one is more important than the other. Jesus himself modeled this kind of balanced commitment. In Luke 4:31-44, we find Jesus moving back and forth between prayer and service. Looking at just one day in his life, we see him teaching in the synagogue, healing people of various diseases, and casting out demons. At the end of this long day, early the next morning, Jesus departed to a deserted place to pray in preparation for another full day of ministry.

A balanced life becomes possible when we commit ourselves to living out our faith. As we were reminded in the first session, commitment is prior to intimacy. Jesus' commitment to his mission led him to ever-increasing intimacy with God, preparing him for the ultimate act of compassion—death on the cross.

All of this is a day-by-day process of growth. Even in the life of Jesus, we can speak of a constantly maturing faith. Luke put it this way: "Jesus increased in wisdom and in years, and in divine and human favor" (Luke 2:52). In our lives, we follow the lead of Jesus as we daily commit ourselves to growing in compassion for others and in intimacy with God. Parents of young children make this kind of commitment even though they cannot know exactly what that commitment will require of them as their children grow up. As parents change diapers, clean up messes, play with and teach a child, the relationship develops, intimacy grows, and commitment unfolds.

Similarly, idealistic youth commit themselves to a year of volunteer service. As they live with people who are poor, hungry, or experiencing violence, they become more aware of what it is like to live on the edge of life, moment by moment. In 1981, Yvonne Dilling volunteered to work in a Honduran refugee camp for Salvadorans fleeing war in their country. One day, frightened people began pouring over the river-border from El Salvador, seeking safety in the camp. The first refugees to arrive told Yvonne that hundreds of people were still waiting to cross the river, mostly women and children who could not make it alone. Salvadoran soldiers patrolled one side, torturing and killing their fellow citizens who were trying to flee. Honduran soldiers patrolled the other side, shooting refugees to stem the flow of people into Honduras. Horrified, Yvonne and a priest ran toward the river to help the people cross, pushing aside the fear of instant death.

This was the most dangerous thing Yvonne had ever done, but she knew that her faith had led her to this very moment. She was determined to help, even in the grip of overwhelming terror. At the river, she quickly slipped into the water and for several hours grabbed hand after hand. She swam back and forth from bank to bank, struggling against swift currents to tote screaming, terrified babies and children to safety on the other side. They dragged her down, pulling her hair and ears to stay above the water.

Suddenly Salvadoran helicopters roared overhead and began firing at them, showering one side of the river with bullets, turning around and strafing the other side. People ran for cover under rocks and trees. Yvonne and the priest had found hiding places for everyone but themselves. They had to keep running around a boulder, always keeping the stone between themselves and the roving helicopter.

Finally, when the helicopter veered off and left, everyone collapsed in relief and utter exhaustion. New volunteers came to help the rest of the people cross to safety. Only when it was over did Yvonne and the others have a chance to think about what had happened. They concluded that the desire to be faithful to their mission overcame the kind of fear that usually immobilizes people. And many lives were saved that day.

For a Purposeful Mission

Being immersed in the lives of those refugees made all the "right answers"—the ones Yvonne had been taught from childhood—come to life for her. The old, familiar scriptures that called her to bring good news to the poor, to proclaim release to the captives, to let the oppressed go free took on new meaning as she stood knee deep in a bullet-splashed river. Such life or death experiences make us realize that Christian commitment goes much deeper than mere assent to a nice-sounding principle or well-ordered program. Commitment is being determined to carry out the purpose that God has for us—now. It will likely be a practical, down-to-earth mission. It will be hard work, immediately at hand.

In verse 43 Jesus told the crowds the purpose of his own mission. He had been traveling in Galilee, teaching and healing. Although the crowds wanted him to stay in Capernaum, he said, "I must proclaim the good news of the kingdom of God to the other cities also; for I was sent for this purpose." Having committed to his all-encompassing purpose and its source, he could extend himself in practical acts of compassion wherever he went.

"Commitment to the Lord in his mission is itself a source of becoming intimately acquainted with him as a person," says Peter J. Henriot. Thus being intimate with God is not just an "out there" or an "in here" experience. It encompasses all of life and all of the people who cross our paths. This is what happened with Jesus. He experienced many people, in various situations, and grew in his understanding of God's purpose for him. He lived with balance, holding together a purposeful mission of compassion and a fruitful, growing relationship with God.

For us to maintain the balance between "doing" and "being" requires discipline. In our full, busy, hectic lives we often convince ourselves that we do not have time for both prayer and action. A new church member was speaking with the pastor about his newfound faith and his desire to live it more intentionally. The pastor suggested that he might try spending about thirty minutes every day in prayer. The new member politely replied that that would be impossible. He proceeded to detail all of the activities that filled his days. The pastor smiled and said, "Oh, I see. That much to do! Maybe you need to spend an *hour* each day in prayer."

Discussion and Action

1. Recall the statement by Henri Nouwen in the third section of this week's Personal Preparation. How did you decide to "waste time with God" this week? In what ways did this become holy time for you? How could such times of being present to the Lord stir you to compassionate action for others?

2. How do you try to maintain balance in your personal life between "doing" and "being"? What things do you do to maintain that balance?

3. What does it mean for you, in practical terms, to "depart . . . into a deserted place" (4:42)? If possible, talk about the last time you did this. Could you describe your aloneness as productive in any way, or as compassionate? Explain.

4. C. S. Lewis, in *Letters to Malcolm,* made this comment about prayer: "Our prayers for others flow more easily than those we offer on our own behalf. . . . One [reason] is that I am often, I believe, praying for others when I should be doing things for them. It's so much easier to pray for a bore than to go and see him." How do you determine when it is best to pray for someone . . . or better to visit her or him?

5. Share your reflections regarding situations in your community that call for compassion. As a result of your sharing and brainstorming, decide on a specific way your group could attempt compassionate action.

6. If you are considering a potential sister-church relationship, work together to devise a list of purposes for the ministry. Spark your thinking by analyzing this purpose statement from the Buena Vista-Bella Vista churches mentioned in the previous session:

Our reasons for becoming partners in ministry are: To be in mutual ministry and mission in sharing the message of salvation and service in Jesus Christ. To learn of ministry and mission approaches utilized in other cultures and congregational settings. To enhance our understanding of the Christian faith as expressed within the cultural setting of each congregation. To build up the body of Christ by the bond of a common love for Jesus, the fellowship of the Holy Spirit, and the fellowship of believers.

3

A 'Doing' that Risks
Luke 9:28-43

Three disciples went to a hilltop with Jesus and directly encountered the living God. Peter was especially moved and suggested an immediate plan of action. But later, when the task before them required healing action, the disciples could not produce. Being on the "mountaintop" kindles spiritual renewal. A growing faith, however, must still risk the possibility of failure in every decision to reach out with compassion.

Personal Preparation

1. Think about how you would characterize the role of risk in your faith journey. When has God's presence in your life compelled you to get off your knees and risk reaching out to others? When have you risked the most for your faith?

2. Reflect on times you have experienced the awesome presence of God, some of the mountain-top experiences in your life. What happened when you came back down from those experiences? What were you led to do then?

3. Read aloud Luke 9:28-43. Imagine being one of the disciples who failed to heal the boy in this story. How would you feel? What questions might you have for Jesus the next time you saw him?

Understanding

When my children were teenagers, I was convinced that the lock on the front door was wired to every television, radio, and sound system in the house. Whenever my son or daughter unlocked the door, noise broke loose and in seconds the house was jumping with sound. The sensory-deadening clamor filled up time and space that might otherwise have allowed them to get to know themselves, to become friends with themselves and with God.

In our busy, noisy world it is often hard to enter those serene spaces where we know we are meeting with God. With all the distractions, we may even, in a sense, become immune to God's presence. That was not the case on the day when Jesus took his three friends up on the mountain. Those disciples had no choice but to enter into the awesome experience of God. Here was an epiphany—unexpected, unplanned, and just a bit terrifying. Peter tried to dilute the intensity of that experience by immediately proposing a building project. For him, the first order of business was to get busy, with anything.

As we have understood from our studies so far, our faith must issue in action in order to be a balanced commitment. But there is a deeper, more subtle layer of insight for us to consider: are we called to just any action that may come to mind? Compassion starts with a genuine encounter with God, and that encounter invariably thrusts us into *risky* action. Peter would have to do much more than build houses.

Not Yet Ready to Risk?

The disciples had been with Jesus for some time, learning from him and growing in their faith. He had called the twelve together and given them power and authority over demons and diseases (9:1). They had experience in doing the very acts of healing that suddenly, after leaving the mountain, they could not do. Jesus' response to these well-equipped but ineffective disciples was, "You faithless and perverse generation, how much longer must I be with you and bear with you?" (9:41).

Why were the disciples unable to exorcise the demon from the boy? Was it because they had grown comfortable with their roles in the Kingdom of God? Whatever the case, these followers of Jesus were incomplete. They needed to learn that an integrated faith in God involves risk, because it constantly invites us into the most difficult situations in people's lives, situations we cannot solve or cure with our own power.

Some scholars have referred to this passage as a portrayal of the "not-yet-ready disciples." There are times each of us feels not yet ready. I think of the well-known spiritual leader and theologian who arranged to have a six-week personal sabbatical at a retreat house. When others at the retreat house learned that this renowned

theologian was in residence, they asked the retreat director to find
out if the theologian would be willing to hold several seminars for
them. The theologian said, "I have no materials with me—no syl-
labus, no commentaries, nothing. I just do not feel prepared to
offer any wisdom or leadership without something to draw from."
The wise retreat director responded, "Why would you even hesitate
to share your wisdom with these young people? After all, God has
been preparing you for this all of your life." But the theologian was
not willing to open up . . . without notes.

Consider Opening Up

We might say that opening up to one another is the first step in a risky
outreach. Suppose, in our covenant group, I tell you of a time I stood
stripped to my soul in God's presence—vulnerable, naked, alone, just
God and I—during a time of personal crisis. Can I trust you with all
that I am, once I let the facade of respectability crumble down around
my feet?

Teresa of Avila, a sixteenth-century Carmelite nun, wrote, "It is
foolish to think that we will enter heaven without entering into ourselves, coming to know our weakness and what we owe God, and
begging for God's mercy." Surely there is risk in meeting God face
to face. Moses knew the risk when he went up on the mountain and
entered the fiery cloud that covered the glory of the Lord (Exod.
24:15-18). Being in God's presence overwhelms us because we find
our innermost self revealed, and there is no place to hide. In the
same way, we risk as we reach out toward others, starting with a vulnerable openness, a determination to be self-revealing with those we
hope to love and be loved by. "Risk and spirituality are lovers," said
Matthew Fox.

One reason we fear to risk in our spiritual journeys is that God
demands the role of primary actor in our unfolding histories. We cannot hope to build our own "dwellings" through personal ingenuity
while building the Kingdom of God by the power of the Spirit. Rather,
our calling is a daily act of risky submission. "Here am I Lord, send
me." Who knows what destination will be inscribed on the trip ticket
of a spiritual journey?

Like the disciples on the Mount of Transfiguration, we too are
being acted upon. We are, in effect, out of control. Maybe we should
give Peter credit for at least attempting a response to God's startling
revelation. He blurted out his desire, "not knowing what he said"
(9:33). Are we any different? Our plans and agendas, even for worthy

service, must often seem naive and foolish to God. Yet growing and maturing in our Christian faith calls for letting go of our imagined control. Just such vulnerability and such risking, showing our true selves before our Lord and our brothers and sisters, is the seedbed of compassion.

Investigate the Avoidance Factor

Beginning in 1987, six major denominations joined the Search Institute and Lilly Endowment in launching a four-year study of religious faith. The study yielded some fascinating information regarding the nature of faith maturity among youth and adults. A "mature faith" was defined as having both horizontal and vertical dimensions. The vertical aspect of faith comes through in "a deep personal relationship with a loving God." The horizontal aspect includes "translating this personal affirmation into acts of love, mercy, and justice." According to Search Institute findings, a mature Christian:
- •trusts and believes,
- •experiences the fruits of faith,
- •integrates faith and life,
- •seeks spiritual growth,
- •experiences and nurtures faith in community,
- •holds life-affirming values,
- •advocates social change, and
- •acts and serves.

We all have seen cartoons of people leaving Sunday morning worship with sighs of relief that their weekly spiritual refueling is once again complete; they can now resume life as usual. The elements of mature Christian faith, as listed above, are not nurtured by a weekly religious pit stop. Growth in compassion is rarely a comfortable, day-trip jaunt through the countryside. For most who dare to sign on, it is more like a river-raft excursion through white water, or a caravan adventure through desert and jungle—all on a one-way ticket.

However described, the journey calls for a lifestyle both that we choose and that we must cultivate. In an article on spiritual renewal, Joan Deeter writes, "The danger in renewal [is that] it won't stop on our knees. . . . As we give more attention to knowing and embodying the spirit of Christ, we will likely find ourselves nudged into new ministries, some we would prefer to avoid."

There's the rub. Many ministries, indeed, we rather would avoid. It is all too easy to turn on the television once again, to fill up our days with noise and busy-ness, while leaving those risky nudgings for another day. As G. K. Chesterton once put it, "The Christian ideal has not been tried and found wanting; it has been found difficult and left untried."

Discussion and Action

1. In your Personal Preparation you reflected on times you experienced God's awesome presence. Share these experiences. Talk about, for example, when you have felt the most overwhelmed, vulnerable, naked, or out of control in God's presence. What happened? How did you handle it?

2. How many times have you sung the hymn phrase "Melt me, mold me, fill me, use me" and yet made an easy response, such as contributing a few cans to the food pantry? Did God ever, one day, call you to do something more risky? What was it? What caused you to be ready to move toward the more vulnerable and risky action?

3. Focus for a moment on the elements of mature Christian faith from the Search Institute findings. Which of the eight marks of faith are especially challenging you at this point in your life? How are you growing in those areas?

4. How would you characterize the avoidance factor in your life right now? What can you share with the group about this aspect of your life? What steps would you like to take to face your responsibilities and answer your callings more directly?

5. Here is a short poem written by Amelia Earhart, an adventurous aviator of the early twentieth century:

Courage is the price that life exacts for granting peace.
The soul that knows it not, knows no release from little
      things;
Knows not the livid loneliness of fear,
Nor mountain heights where bitter joy can hear
The sound of wings.

In your opinion, what part does courage play in a life of compassion? How is the courage that Amelia spoke of like, and unlike, Christian courage? What act of courage might your group consider in the weeks ahead?

6. In your sister-church exploration, a first step is to ask your pastor if she or he is interested in learning about your denomination's work in this area. Designate someone in your group to contact your pastor this week and to report back at your next meeting. Find out if your pastor can give you the name and telephone number of the person in your district, region, or denominational headquarters who would have suggestions about how to find a sister-church.

4

The Fear Is Real
Luke 12:1-12

Having encountered the hostility of the religious leaders, Jesus began to prepare his followers for the inevitable persecutions to come. They must beware the temptation to travel incognito, as though they were not members of his new order. The fear would be real, but they could trust in God's care for them, care from the one who remembers even the sparrows.

Personal Preparation

1. Read Luke 12:1-12. What phrases or images "jump out" at you as you read this scripture?
2. Have you ever been in a situation in which you pretended not to be a Christian? Why did you do so?
3. When you think of reaching out with compassion, what kinds of fears begin to surface? Spend some moments feeling those fears. Are there any connections to fears and events from your childhood?

Understanding

I know a church that prides itself on being a loving and caring congregation. One of the women in that congregation developed a degenerative brain disease. Her illness caused her to become careless about her personal hygiene and appearance. She exuded a terrible body odor and always looked unkempt. Other members of the church stopped sitting near the woman. They complained and gossiped about her. One person suggested that the pastor ask her to stay home because she was so offensive to others. The woman became more and more isolated in the midst of her Christian community.

Finally, two women in the congregation went to the woman to talk with her about her problem and to help her with her personal needs. They arranged to care for her in the most intimate and loving ways. They began washing and setting her hair. They bathed her regularly. They spent time talking with her and reading books to her. These two were no longer willing to gossip about this woman or wish she would just go away. They decided to become the loving and caring people they wanted to be, once they overcame their basic fears.

Confronting Our Fear

In the previous chapter of Luke, Jesus launched one of his harshest attacks on the hypocrisy of the community's religious leaders (see the "six woes" of Luke 11:37-54). Later in this session's passage, Jesus helped his disciples recognize a type of fearful hypocrisy that could ensnare them as well. They might be tempted, in the face of future persecution, to deny their connection to the Lord. They had to decide where they stood. Would they continue to side with Jesus, even in public?

Applications of Jesus' words extend far beyond the early disciples. Certainly Jesus also speaks to our own fears today, the fears that can keep us from being the community of compassion we wish to be. And it is mostly fear, rather than calculated unkindness, that keeps us at bay, even in the case of the malodorous woman. Brought into contact with her, any of us might wonder, suppose she really wants to be my friend? How much would I have to give? Who would see us together? What if I catch her disease? Perhaps our deepest concern might surface: Suppose my Christian commitment turns out to be mostly drudgery after all, with precious little glory attached?

In light of such understandable fears, are you, like me, ever tempted to be a "closet" Christian? Fear is a powerful thing. In most of our relationships—in our families, churches, and neighborhoods—there are some things we want to hide. That is the kind of hypocrisy Jesus must have seen in the Pharisees when he warned his disciples, "Beware of the yeast of the Pharisees, that is, their hypocrisy" (12:1). Any person can fall into a religion of mere habit that offers only lip service to faithful living. Jesus said that such a fake lifestyle would be uncovered. Faithfulness allows for no more secrets.

Harmful secrets abound in our society, especially in families that experience violence and abuse. When adults or children suffer abuse, the abuser often threatens, "Don't you dare tell!" Yet only as these terrible secrets come to light can healing start. Most of us are only beginning to learn how to offer compassion to people caught in a web of harmful secrets. It is so much easier to pretend that abusive or violent situations do not happen among us. To hear such stories makes us fearful and sad; therefore we keep one another at arm's length and fail to enter deeply into our true concerns. Sometimes it seems just too painful. Many years ago I saw this reluctance horribly demonstrated. Two little girls attended worship and Sunday school each week. They were quiet and well behaved, always neatly dressed, yet they harbored a terrible secret. The older sister was sexually molested regularly by her father. Sunday morning worship was a time of sanctuary for her, and she always brought her younger sister along to protect her from similar abuse. It was not until many years later that this girl, now a woman, was able to reveal her secret and begin to experience healing. In one way or another, all of us must confront our fears and uncover the truth if healing and compassion are to blossom.

Uncovering the Truth . . . and Our Faith

How can we help compassionately uncover the lies that prevent intimacy? Or, to ask the question another way, how can we fearlessly uncover the truth of our faith in Jesus? Melissa A. Miller in her book *Family Violence: The Compassionate Church Responds,* offered this suggestion: "It is crucial to maintain our life-sustaining connection to God when journeying through stormy waters. . . . The simplest acts of our faith journey—prayer and reflection on the Bible and God's word—preserve us." These simple acts open us to the Holy Spirit.

The hypocrisy revealed in Luke 12:4-12 was that followers of Jesus were pretending not to be faithful disciples. Why would any disciple attempt to cover up his or her faith? Would someone pretend not to be a disciple because of the fear of inconvenience, unpopularity, ridicule, or persecution? Jesus told us that we could move through such fears if we put our trust in God. When we openly confess our faith rather than trying to hide it, we are promised that the Holy Spirit will be with us in the midst of our worries and our fears. Then the prayer of Peter Marshall can be answered in our lives: "Give to us clear vision that we may know where to stand and what to stand for—because unless we stand for something, we shall fall for anything."

The Spirit will lead us to live and speak the truth where oppression and violence have kept it hidden. "The Holy Spirit will teach you at that very hour what you ought to say" (12:12). Cliff Kindy, as a member of a Christian Peacemaker Team practicing a nonviolent presence in Israeli-occupied territories, has on several occasions traveled from his home in Indiana to live with Palestinian families for some weeks. He told about an evening with one host family in a refugee camp in Gaza:

> It is a few minutes before 9 p.m. curfew, and Hashim and I shower and dress for bed. Hashim's brother Nassir, his wife, and two of his four children come into Hashim's room where we sit on the pads at the foot of the bed, watching TV and talking. . . . Then Hashim, with flashes of his cigarette lighter, lights my way upstairs to my balcony bed pad. As I lie down, pondering the experience of another day in a new land, the sound of footsteps on the sandy street below reaches my sleeping place next to Alla, one of Hashim's other brothers.
>
> Who is running loose after curfew? . . . My head peeks above the balcony edge and drops with a flutter. Maybe six soldiers break the curfew of the night. What is the meaning? I reach to Alla's bed, shake his arm and barely mouth my "Shhh! Soldiers!" I caution him to remain low, and I point. He nods his head, believing in the face of my disbelief. In a moment the feet move back along the street and into the darkness. We check in all directions to see if they are really gone. In my English and his Arabic we mutter about the dream scene below. At least our house is safe for the moment. . . .
>
> But more footsteps, sandaled ones this time, break into my racing brain, steps echoing through empty rooms. It is Hashim, with almost a crazy smile twitching his lips. "They took my brother Nassir," he says.
>
> I sit, speechless, recognizing the reality that slaps its tail across my face. They had crossed the wall, silent as rats, and entered his bedroom. Nassir and his wife were in bed and their four children scattered on pads around the bed and outside the room. "Are you Nassir?" they asked. With affirmation, he rose. He was then hooded, his hands tied with cutting plastic behind his back, and led away.
>
> Hashim and I talk and watch the night, its silence now broken only by distant military vehicles, their searchlights probing the Palestinian night. He bids me later, "Sleep well; don't think." I don't sleep well. My racing thoughts raise me on cautious knees at every sound whispering

through the streets below. But the rustle is only of a rat, running loose in the night.

Whenever we reveal or uncover what others would prefer to keep hidden, someone will become angry. We must proceed, nevertheless. In this particular situation, Cliff's presence meant that the soldiers' secret nighttime arrests would now be known beyond the boundaries of the refugee camp. To reveal this kind of secret out of one's Christian conviction is terrifyingly dangerous. At such times we need to hold close to our hearts the precious words of Jesus: "Do not be afraid" (12:32). "Do not worry" (12:11). With our souls in his care, even death cannot defeat us.

Discussion and Action

1. Share some stories about times you have pretended to be someone you were not. Encourage humor. Then refer to Personal Preparation question 2. Share together about times it was hard to admit being a Christian.

2. Read Matthew 10:18-20, Mark 13:11, and Luke 21:14-15. In what ways could these scriptures and today's text encourage people fearful of living out their faith?

3. Read Exodus 4:10-13, using two readers who take the parts of Moses and the Lord. Have you ever been like Moses, wanting to resist God's call and keep your gifts hidden from others? What fears lay behind Moses' resistance? What fears lie behind your resistance?

4. How is your congregation helping to break down the barriers that allow people to keep harmful secrets? How does your covenant group break down barriers of secrecy?

5. How do you apply these words of Jesus personally: "Do not be afraid. Do not worry"? What makes it difficult not to be afraid? Why is it hard not to worry?

6. Respond to the statement that Christian living may involve "drudgery . . . with precious little glory attached." How do you keep going in your witness and ministry when exhaustion hits? What physical, emotional, and spiritual activities refresh you?

7. If you have designated someone to contact your pastor about a sister-church partnership, ask for a report. If you have your pastor's support, do some preliminary work to define your

church's "culture"—its membership makeup, biblical literacy, education levels, cross-cultural exposure, etc. Then discuss the types of cross-cultural experiences that could benefit you. Consider potential forms of fellowship across national, racial, geographic, or socioeconomic barriers.

In your discussion, remember that a sister-church relationship is a mutual ministry with neither congregation having any sense of "rescuing" the other. Both congregations have something to give as they seek a practical expression of unity in the body of Christ.

5

Definitely Unconventional
Luke 13:10-17

While Jesus was teaching in the synagogue, a diseased woman entered. Ignoring the traditional rules of the Sabbath, Jesus healed the woman and sparked a controversy among the onlookers. His action is controversial for us, as well, because we often fear the unconventional. Yet Jesus calls us to do what is loving and right, even if it means breaking a lesser law.

Personal Preparation

1. Read Luke 13:10-17. How did each character in this passage react to Jesus' healing actions? With which of the characters do you most closely identify? How? Why?
2. Recall a time when you felt a need to play the "savior" with a loved one. Think about what happened when such a role was taken away, perhaps by a change that made our loved one stronger.
3. If you were invited to come to Jesus with your own crippling malady, what would it be? How would your life change if that malady were healed or removed? How would your life change if you were granted a greater measure of acceptance?

Understanding

Children were leading the Sunday morning service, dramatizing the woman's miraculous healing. Marie, a petite eleven-year-old, slowly entered the chancel, bending over, supporting herself with a cane. When Jesus called out and said, "Woman, you are set free!" (13:12), Marie responded immediately. She stood up straight and shouted, "Praise

God!" at the top of her lungs. Then she sprang into non-stop cartwheels, whirling head over heels, right down the center aisle of the sanctuary! That must have been the way this woman felt after eighteen years of being bent double, always forced to look at the ground. Now she could take her rightful place in her family and community. Jesus had, indeed, set her free.

Creating a Controversy

By healing the woman, however, Jesus upset a delicate balance. She had come merely to worship. She made no request for healing, had not complained. But Jesus, when he saw her, was moved to compassion and action. According to one Bible commentator, "The peace of the way things have always been is shattered by the word and deed of Jesus. If helping a stooped woman creates a crisis, then crisis it has to be."

Even though no one would have admitted to wanting the woman to continue suffering, the response to her healing was mixed. Some "opponents" (13:17) were indignant because Jesus did not follow the traditional no-work rules of the Sabbath. Even the leader of the synagogue kept saying not just once, but many times: "There are six days on which work ought to be done," for heaven's sake! "Come on those days and be cured, and not on the Sabbath day" (13:14). There are certain ways to act and be on the Sabbath; unfortunately, these ways do not always lead along the pathway of love.

Of course, Jesus and the synagogue leader both wanted what was right. They both wanted to follow the law *and* to help other people. We, too, want to reach out and help others but often on our own terms, just like the ruler of the synagogue. Sometimes our fear of change keeps people bent over and in bondage. Sometimes our focus on the rules works against compassionate outreach. We want to help the poor, *if* they follow our rules. We will assist welfare mothers, *if* they get a job and have no more children. We will feed the hungry, *if* they are properly thankful.

All of these may be appropriate goals, but are they prerequisites for compassion? Jesus did not have a list of expectations for this hurting woman to fulfill before he provided healing. His challenge to all of us is to move compassion beyond the law, beyond our own expectations, no matter how controversial the outcome.

Coping with Change

The woman experienced an amazing change in her life. Can you imagine what it must have been like? We think immediately of the joy, the happiness, the gratitude we would feel. But there is more than one side to every occasion of change. How do you suppose the woman's family and neighbors reacted after the euphoria of the miracle day subsided? How did husband, children, grandchildren, and friends feel in the next week or next month when they found their wife, mother, grandmother, friend no longer bent double—*when they found that she no longer needed so much help from them?*

Even positive change is hard to accept when it upsets a comfortable, familiar balance of relationships. Think about what happens in families as children grow and move from one stage in life to another. When children can finally feed themselves, when at last they enter school, when they choose "strange" friends and music, when they get that first job, when they move away from home, when they start raising grandchildren in all the "wrong" ways. Such changes affect everyone in the family and demand adjustments by all.

Perhaps this woman's family and friends did not even recognize her when she walked back into the old neighborhood. Who could even imagine her with head held high, the sunshine lighting up her face? We have all experienced something similar. A child who has been irresponsible, never picking up after herself, suddenly cleans her room without being reminded. Her parents are amazed. *What brought about this surprising new behavior?* A young boy who only bathes and combs his hair under protest now miraculously takes a fastidious interest in his appearance. *Okay, so who's the new girlfriend?* A man whose wife and family have been brutalized by his alcoholism seems like a new person because of treatment and continuing recovery. *Can we really trust him now with this new confidence . . . and potential independence? Will he still need us?*

With those questions in our minds, with the challenge of accepting the change in relationships and behavior, we often find it easier to keep things the way they were. There is security in the conventional, a comfortable safety of the predictable. Yet to advocate for compassion and justice, even when it may be unpopular, difficult, or illegal, may be the only way to fulfill love's obligations. Like Jesus, sometimes we must counter the conventional.

Countering the Conventional

A retired clergywoman serves in a volunteer ministry to prisoners on death row. She visits regularly, listens, shares the gospel, prays with all who are willing to meet with her. She maintains contact with the prisoners' families and advocates for legislative change on their behalf. Not everyone who knows of this ministry supports it. To many people, it seems a waste of time when there are so many other "real" needs in this world. After all, these criminals deserve the punishment for the evil acts they have committed.

This rugged, spunky lady sees beyond a vision of our world that, at its best, offers only an "eye for an eye" existence. To her, these death-row prisoners have all of the human needs for companionship, friendship, and emotional support that anyone outside the gray prison walls has. Yes, these men and women live their day-to-day existence in a prison, but even there, they are still children of God.

As I think about compassionate, controversial ministry, I have to ask in what ways I will be tempted by the rules today, lured by the conventional, unwilling to question "the way we have always done it." I know I will always face conflicts between the call to administer proper justice and to extend unconditional love. But I also know that my supreme example, Jesus, often moved beyond the letter of the law to offer healing. He was compelled by a higher vision. The question for Jesus was not whether an act was conventional or controversial, legal or illegal. Rather the question was, how can I fulfill my commitment to God in this situation? It is the same question for you and me, and our responses have cartwheel-inducing potential.

Discussion and Action

1. Discuss your responses to the first question of Personal Preparation. Share your thinking about the biblical characters' reactions to the woman's healing, and tell about your own identification with these characters.
2. Refer to the third Personal Preparation question. Invite volunteers to talk about any physical or emotional "crippling" they might bring to an incarnate Jesus. In general, do we need more healing or more acceptance of such things in our lives? Explain.
3. Are there times when our spiritual focus works against compassion today, as it did for the leader of the synagogue? Name some of the possible times and places in which a spiritual focus could work against compassion.
4. What are some ways in which our resistance to change keeps people "bent over"? When have you seen this happen?
5. When might advocating for justice and compassion in illegal ways be "the only way to fulfill love's obligations"?

Have you ever had to break a law to serve a higher law? What happened?

6. When have you appreciated the safety of the predictable the most? In what ways is your covenant group appropriately safe and predictable? Brainstorm some less safe ways that your group could reach out in the weeks ahead.

7. As you continue to explore the sister-church idea, add to the preliminary self-assessment you did in the last session. Develop a list of gifts, resources, and needs of your congregation. If you do not have a potential sister-church to contact yet, this is still a preparatory time for you to discover what things you would be able to give and receive in such a relationship. Spark your thinking by looking through the "Get Acquainted" suggestions listed in General Resources.

6

It Costs *What?*
Luke 14:25-35

Large crowds traveled with Jesus, enjoying the sights and sounds of successful ministry. How many in the crowd knew that they were journeying with a young martyr-to-be? How many recognized that there is a price tag attached to following the Savior? Even today, how many of us have counted the cost?

Personal Preparation

1. Read Luke 14:25-35. What is the cutting edge for you in counting the cost of discipleship?
2. Recall the commitment you made in becoming a part of your church. How long did it take you to decide on membership? What kinds of promises did you make in front of the church members? How well have you upheld those promises so far?
3. Choose a hymn that has a special meaning for you as you remember your confession of faith or use the hymn "Living for Jesus" (in General Sharing and Prayer Resources). Reread the words in a moment of silence. Be prepared to read the words of the hymn to your group or sing it together.

Understanding

In their book *Resident Aliens,* William Willimon and Stanley Hauerwas tell the story of a southern town confronting school integration in the '60s. The townspeople gathered in the high school gym to protest the court's order to integrate. Most of the people were angry and the room seethed with hatred. The Baptist minister, much loved and respected in the community for many years, sat in the front row.

He listened to the speeches for a while and then strode to the podium. "I am ashamed," he said. "I have labored here through much of my life. I have baptized, preached to, and counseled with many in this room. I might have thought that my preaching of the Gospel—the word of God—had done some good. But tonight I think differently. I am hurt and ashamed of you and might have expected more." He left the podium and walked resolutely toward the back door, his fiery eyes fixing on any who dared to look up at him.

Perhaps many people in the crowd that night thought that their pastor's expectations were too high. Many could say, after all, that they had been Christians for years and had done much good in the church and community. Now something more was demanded. Many were not willing to pay the price, to let go of their prejudices in order to embrace a new way of living. When the pastor stood up to speak, he could not know how the crowd would react, but his commitment demanded that he move out of the comfort zone—and try to move others out of it, too.

Let us not be too hard on the crowd gathered in that gym so many years ago. Which of us has not felt the same call to give up or give in for the sake of Jesus—and resisted that call? With that call comes the stinging reminder that we have not entered into our journey with Jesus on the basis of a cheap grace. We have felt that sting and will feel it again.

But others have heard the call and immediately said, "Yes, Jesus!" In a sense, they needed more "holy reluctance." Being too quick and too willing, they did not consider the full cost of true discipleship.

Too Willing?

Like the Baptist preacher, Jesus knew that many who followed did not completely understand the demanding implications of the gospel message. They wanted the hope, the joy, the peace, the promise, but they preferred to ignore or avoid the pain, the sorrow, and the cross.

This section in Luke moves us abruptly from Jesus' semi-private teachings in a house to statements he offered to "the crowds." It is a brief section dealing with teachings about the nature of true discipleship. The key to understanding it is to recognize that here Jesus was not facing the people's reluctance to follow him. Rather, he spoke to those who were all too willing to sign on with him. William Barclay put it this way: "It is possible to be a follower of Jesus without being a disciple; to be a camp-follower without being a soldier of the king; to be a hanger-on in some great work without pulling one's weight."

So Jesus raised the crucial questions: Have you considered the price of discipleship—just as a builder estimates the cost of a construction project? Have you thought about the inevitable opposition you will face—just as a warring king ponders the strength of his enemy?

Of course, it is hard for any of us to ask about the cost of something when it is so new and shiny and appealing. Exactly at such a time Jesus asked his followers to consider the cost of discipleship. He was enjoying the height of his popularity as an itinerant preacher in the Judean countryside. Great crowds flocked after him as he preached a message of good news and hope to an oppressed people, healing their sick. They would have followed him anywhere, done whatever he asked . . . or so they believed.

It was exciting to be a part of this movement, to follow Jesus across the countryside day by day, quoting his wonderful sayings, retelling his teachings, describing his latest miracle. It was all so full of love and promise and hope. How shocking then, when Jesus turned and said, "Whoever comes to me and does not hate father and mother, wife and children, brothers and sisters, yes, and even life itself, cannot be my disciple" (14:26).

Willing to Be Unpopular?

Sometimes compassion requires taking up an unpopular cause that will make our priorities stand out in stark relief. This is at least part of the cost Jesus asserted. At such times it may seem we are betraying even our loved ones. That is why Jesus, in verse 26, said that our commitment would seem like hatred for our family, and for our own life. To "hate," in this verse, is an expression that has the meaning of "turning away from." It holds little of the bitter emotional flavor that we associate with our angry statement, "I hate you!" As Bible commentator Fred Craddock explains, "What is demanded of disciples is that in the network of many loyalties in which all of us live, the claim of Christ and the gospel not only takes precedence but, in fact redefines the others. This can and will necessarily involve some detaching, some turning away."

How can we detach, turn away, when we live in a society that constantly invites us only to consider what we *want* rather than what we must *pay?* We use our credit cards and are rewarded when the bank raises our line of credit. Yet "credit" is just a nice way of saying "debt." Is there a nice way of saying "cross"? Consider the irony of that—a horrible instrument of torture having become for so many a dainty piece of jewelry!

Even in the church we prefer to be comfortable and lighthearted rather than take seriously the weight of shouldering the cross. How is it in your congregation? Does your pastor speak of the cost of following Christ? Many churches, in their concern for bringing in new members, fail to teach the marks of discipleship. How many lessons have you heard lately on tithing, living a simple life, being a steward of all of life, or doing radical peacemaking? Is it possible to encourage a deepening faith when life in Jesus Christ as we know it is so . . . comfortable?

Writer Jess Moody drew the contrast between a comfortable and a costly compassion: "Compassion is not a snob gone slumming. Anybody can salve his conscience by an occasional foray into knitting for the retirement home. Did you ever take a real trip down inside the broken heart of a friend? To feel the sob of the soul—the raw, red crucible of emotional agony? To have this become almost as much yours as that of your soul-crushed neighbor? Then, to sit down with him—and silently weep? This is the beginning of compassion." To align ourselves with the hurting, the weak, the ones who cannot pay us back (see Luke 14:12-14) will usually make us less popular than we would like to be. When it comes to letting go of our egos, that costs us.

Willing to "Give Up"?

Jesus wanted the crowds to know what it meant to follow him, perhaps because the people were so unclear as to the kind of leader he truly was. We are often not much clearer today, even with the perspective of an additional two thousand years. "We have turned Jesus into a Warm Fuzzy," wrote William J. O'Malley, who teaches religion at a high school in Rochester, New York. O'Malley quoted from one typical student's reflections on God: "I had—and still have to some degree—the assumption that you can treat God like a wimp. Like I can do whatever I want, and He'll just forget about it, no matter how I really feel. . . . It really isn't possible to have a relationship with a wimpy God."

Verse 33 is a decidedly un-wimpy summary of discipleship! "So therefore, none of you can become my disciple if you do not give up all your possessions." How can we handle this statement? Perhaps you saw the movie *The End,* in which Burt Reynolds played a man attempting suicide. Through a comedy of errors and misunderstandings, none of his attempts ever met with success. Finally he swam far out into the ocean, and then had a change of heart. He suddenly wanted to live! He started the long swim back to shore, praying fervently as he went, "Lord, save me! I promise I'll be a better father . . . if you'll only save me. I'll obey the Ten Commandments: Thou shalt not kill. Thou shalt not steal. Thou shalt . . . ? Okay, I'll learn the Ten Commandments, God, if you'll only help me get to shore. I'll give fifty percent of my income to the church—gross income."

As he neared the shore, his prayers became less fervent: "I'll give forty percent of my income Lord . . . thirty percent . . . twenty percent . . . ten percent." And as his feet finally touched bottom, he added, "That's ten percent of my *net* income."

Obviously our attitude is the key to genuine self-sacrifice, because in the final analysis, giving up is not a demand but an opportunity. As counselor and writer Gerald May said, "God brings into our lives the *loss* of what we have been holding onto, what identifies us, what is saving our ego. We are forced to let it go and given the opportunity to just *be* in His love."

Discussion and Action

1. Share your reflections from Personal Preparation number 1. What do you, personally, need to consider in counting the cost of discipleship? What relationships, possessions, or attitudes could you loosen your grip on in order to follow Jesus more faithfully?

2. What do you think Jesus meant when he said, "Whoever does not carry the cross and follow me cannot be my disciple" (14:27)? Would you characterize yourself as a disciple at this moment? Why?

3. What do you think is meant by "holy reluctance"? When have you needed more—or less—of that quality in your own life?

4. In what ways do your congregation and your covenant group challenge their members to move beyond the comfort level in their faith? How do people react to these challenges?

5. As we encounter Christ, we feel a call upon our lives, a bittersweet summons to commitment that theologian-martyr Dietrich Bonhoeffer characterized this way: "When Christ calls a man [or woman], he bids [them] come and die." What qualities of dying have you discovered in the call of God upon your own life?

6. Spend some time challenging one another to make some costly personal decisions. Specify a definite period of time. For example, some may choose to tithe, serve in a local soup

kitchen, volunteer at a shelter for the homeless, help with the children's nursery, or read to a nursing home resident. Consider any creative idea.

7. Take another step in pursuing a sister-church relationship. Consider forming a committee to check on potential congregational interest in the idea. Be sure you have your pastor's full support. Work together on ideas for announcing how church members could express interest. For example, could you use a sign-up sheet for a low-key informational gathering?

7

Keep on Knocking
Luke 18:1-8

*According to Jesus, God is a just judge who answers the
persistent seeker. Although it is easy to lose heart when
our petitions go unanswered, we can trust that God will
come through. Holding to our faith in trying circumstances prepares us to help compassionately when others
face similar trials.*

Personal Preparation

1. Read Luke 18:1-8 and Habakkuk 1:1-2 and 2:2-3. What do
   you learn about persistence in prayer and faith from these
   passages?
2. When have you prayed for something persistently? How was
   your prayer answered?
3. Think about how learning to "wait on God" could make you
   a more compassionate person. When has this happened in
   your life?

Understanding

An elderly African American minister read this parable of the Unjust
Judge and gave a one-sentence interpretation: "Until you have stood
for years knocking at a locked door, your knuckles bleeding, you do
not really know what prayer is."

The widow in Jesus' parable kept knocking . . . and waiting. She
expected that justice would someday be done, that an answer would
come. The unjust judge had refused to try her case fairly, no doubt thinking to himself, "Why should I waste my time with her? She's only a poor
widow with no social status, no money, no political clout." But the

widow continued to return, acting as if the judge had never said no to her pleas. Finally, the man gave her a fair judgment—just to get rid of her.

Jesus wanted all of his followers to be persistent in their prayers and petitions to God, but not because God is unjust or because God does not already know our needs and our desires. Persistent and patient waiting in prayer is for *our* benefit, not for God's.

Delayed Benefits

What are some of the benefits of waiting and not losing heart (18:1)? Here are two possibilities. First, sometimes delayed answers *give us time to purify our motives.* As we wait, we can discover how to bring our requests more in line with God's will. This happened with a young girl I know. She prayed daily to be more popular in her class at school. However, she gradually began to realize that, in order to be popular, she had to make friends. And to make friends, she had to be a friend. Her prayer changed from "Make me popular" to "Help me become a better friend to my classmates." If we are persistent in praying, likely we will experience similar adjustments in our motives and goals. Waiting, then, is actually an opportunity to become transformed in our inner being—to become the kind of person who can handle the creative, unexpected divine answer when it comes.

Second, unanswered prayers can *intensify our desire for an answer to come,* until there is no doubt in our minds that we sincerely want the thing for which we pray. Many centuries ago, when a young man wished to become a monk, he showed up at the door of the monastery and knocked. The porter was instructed to turn away all applicants . . . at first. If the monk-to-be knocked again and again, and looked as if he would not budge, then he was admitted. Once inside, he would have to apply his hands and back to some of the most laborious and menial jobs in the house. All this was done as a test. Either the desire for a monastic life would increase or, under the burden of various trials, it would wither away. Since *being* a monk was difficult, *becoming* one would have to be difficult, as well.

Difficult Business

Waiting can clarify our motives and intensify our desires for our prayers to be answered, but it is tough to wait. It is a difficult business to determine to live by faith even when God is silent. At the close of his parable, Jesus asked, "When the Son of Man comes, will he find faith on earth?" (18:8) Will anyone still be praying? Or will they have given up by then?

We all experience times of depleted faith. As someone once said, "All the faithful have also been faith-empty at some time." Ignatius of Loyola was one of the saints of the church who pushed on through the occasional "faith-empty" wilderness. After converting to Christianity, Ignatius began praying in caves near his home. It was a joy to him. Then something changed, and he no longer felt God's presence; his heart seemed to turn to ice when he tried to pray. He went on an eight-day fast to try to regain God's favor, but God remained distant. "How long, O God?" he prayed. "Hasten, Lord, to help me." Still God seemed far away, and Ignatius' faith wavered.

The young convert persisted in his prayers even when God seemed not to hear. And one day, as suddenly as it had come upon him, the icy winter of his soul thawed and spiritual springtime blossomed within. The length of our waiting is rarely a measure of our faith's intensity or depth. Rather, the wait displays God's perfect timing at work. "It remains the unavoidable truth that [this story in Luke presents] prayer as continual and persistent, hurling its petitions against long periods of silence," said Bible commentator Fred Craddock. "The human experience is one of delay . . . even while acknowledging the mystery of God's ways."

Habakkuk, a little-known Hebrew prophet, knew about God's silence and about unanswered prayer. Having seen his people cruelly treated for decades, his question was, "O LORD, how long?" (Hab. 1:2) God's answer was, "Be patient and wait." Habakkuk asked his question in the seventh century B.C.E., when the Chaldeans were invading the land of Judah, bringing violence, destruction, and suffering to the people. "O LORD, how long shall I cry for help, and you will not listen?" cried Habakkuk. "Why do you make me see wrongdoing and look at trouble?" (1:2-3).

The prophet's demands resounded with perplexity and frustration. Why did God permit wrong and evil to overcome righteousness and good? Yet God's eventual response would hardly satisfy one impatient for change: Your vision of better times will surely come to pass in its own time . . . in God's time. And if that time seems a little slow in coming, just wait. Or, as the Moffatt translation of Habakkuk 2:3 reads:

The vision has its own appointed hour;
it ripens, it will flower;
for it is sure, and it will not be late.

Defeat Burnout

Waiting is stressful, especially for Type A personalities, our societies "producers," and those in the helping professions. A great deal has been written in recent years about burnout in these folks. Teachers burn out, church volunteers burn out, parents burn out, pastors burn out. People reaching out to others suffer "compassion fatigue." Virtually anyone can reach this point of weariness and dissatisfaction with life. Expensive workshops and popular books tell us how to defeat or cure the problem. Yet, for the person who feels burned out, helpful hints seem to be too little, too late. The question that comes to mind might have been Habakkuk's: "How long will this weariness persist? How long until renewed energy and enthusiasm return to my life? How long can I remain persistent in commitment and prayer? How long, O God?"

Which of us has not wrestled with God during times of spiritual dryness? We ask, "Why? Why *me?* How *long?*" The opportunity to bring our cries, our questions, and our needs to God is a gift. We can name the anger, the frustrations. We can rail at God. A persistent prayer that will not give up on the relationship with God—even when our answer seems long in coming—enables us to live in love rather than burnout. Those times of waiting are the times when God is especially close. "It is when things go wrong," wrote Madeleine L'Engle, "when good things do not happen, when our prayers seem to have been lost, that God is most present. We do not need the sheltering wings when things go smoothly. We are closest to God in the darkness, stumbling along blindly."

A few years ago a pastor and his wife were thrust into crisis when they learned that their young adult son was dying of AIDS. Not only did they have to deal with the reality of his disease and his impending death, they also struggled with the news that he was homosexual. They wondered how to pray during such a sad, chaotic, complicated time. Yet their prayers continued, even when the words did not come to them.

Following their son's death, they still found no easy answers but they began to see themselves on a journey of compassion as they cared for their son and for other AIDS sufferers. They continued their life of prayer while easing the pain of patients dying difficult and lonely deaths.

Perhaps our impatience with God's tardiness and unexpected manner of answering prayer reveals our limited understanding of prayer itself. We tend to make the answer to prayer our primary objective, but it is the relationship we really need—the speaking to God, the coming to God, the learning to trust in an ever-present Presence. Persistence in prayer builds our relationship with God and keeps us faithful. When we commit to following Christ, we are not called to succeed, necessarily, in solving the problems of homelessness, poverty, hunger, racism, violence, or war. We are called only to be faithful during the journey, as each step becomes clear to us. Along the way Jesus asks us, as he did the early disciples, "When the Son of Man comes, will he find any who are faithful?"

Discussion and Action

1. Some people experience prayer as a kind of magic that gives them answers to life's problems. In this parable Jesus presents prayer as asking, seeking, knocking, and waiting—with answers slow in coming and often unclear. Think of something for which you have prayed earnestly in the last six months. Describe the experience of persistent prayer.

2. Discuss what the two passages in Luke and Habakkuk teach about persistence in prayer. Then read 1 Thessalonians 5:16-18. In your opinion, what does it mean to "pray without ceasing"? How have you attempted to pray this way in the past? What has been difficult or easy for you about persistent prayer?

3. Sometimes we hurriedly go through the motions of prayer, or we find ourselves in desperate situations and become frightened into praying. How do we expect God to answer us in such situations?

4. Have you ever experienced "compassion fatigue"? What is it like? Talk about ways you can help yourselves and each other avoid burnout.

5. Think about the pastor and his wife as they prayed for their AIDS-suffering son. They did not know what to say. Have you ever felt the same loss of words before God? What did you do? Now respond to this quote by Victor Hugo: "Certain thoughts are prayers. There are moments when, whatever be the attitude of the body, the soul is on its knees." Can you relate to this statement?

6. How would you respond to a new believer in your church who is going through a spiritual desert, as in the story about Ignatius of Loyola? What would you say if she asked, "Why is there so much promise of answered prayers in the Bible— but it never seems to happen in my life?"

7. Take action on one of the ideas you developed in the last session for assessing congregational interest in a sister-church relationship.

8

Welcome, Lord!
Luke 19:1-10

A little man could not see over the crowd. Jesus was coming, and the man wanted to get a glimpse of him. Did the man expect the celebrity to stop and say, "Let's go over to your house"? Probably not, but that is how salvation works. We want to see, we want to find out. We hear a knock on the door. We let the Savior come in.

Personal Preparation

1. Read Luke 19:1-10. Why do you think Zacchaeus wanted to see Jesus? When have you felt like climbing a tree to see Jesus? What extraordinary effort was required? Were you able to see him more clearly?

2. Reflect on what salvation means to you. What experiences and/or people helped prepare you to receive salvation? In what ways would you characterize salvation as easy or hard?

3. Do you understand yourself as "one who is a sinner" (19:7)? How does your response to this question affect your self-esteem? Be ready to talk about your response in the group meeting.

Understanding

Seven-year-old Jane yawned as she explained to her school teacher, "I'm tired today because we are having a revival at our church, and last night I could not go home to bed until I got salvation. It's hard to get salvation! But finally I did and I could go to bed." We may wonder about Jane's understanding of salvation, but how many of us know what Jesus meant when he said, "Today salvation has come to this house" (19:9)?

Introducing . . . Salvation!

Webster's dictionary defines salvation as "deliverance from the power and effects of sin." As often as we have heard the phrase "saved from sin," we may still be a bit unclear about its real-life implications. The story of Zaccheus can help us understand because it demonstrates salvation's connection to compassion, as Jesus reached out to one so hated. The story is a refresher course in a subject we may assume we have already mastered. There are at least five aspects of salvation shining through in this story, truths important for us to remember as we attempt to reach out to a hurting world.

First, salvation is *an invitation to a process.* More than something we "get" (as little Jane did), it is an invitation to a lifelong process of change. Jesus saw Zaccheus in the tree and invited himself to the tax collector's home. Is this not salvation in a nutshell? Jesus invites himself into our lives, not immediately telling us what is right or wrong but simply offering himself for our acceptance.

Then the changing begins. Frederick Buechner, in his book *Wishful Thinking,* emphasizes the sanctifying process that must follow our initial acceptance of the invitation: "Paul's word for [the] gradual transformation of a sow's ear into a silk purse is sanctification, and he sees it as the second stage in the process of salvation. Being sanctified is a long and painful stage because with part of themselves sinners prefer their sin, just as with part of himself the beast prefers his glistening snout and curved tusks. Many drop out with the job hardly more than begun, and among those who stay with it there are few if any who don't drag their feet most of the way." Clearly, salvation involves process. With Christ settling down to dwell in our house, how could it be otherwise?

Second, salvation is *extended to sinners.* Although Jesus was eager to stay at the home of Zaccheus, Luke tells us that everyone who saw this began to grumble about it. "He has gone to be the guest of one who is a sinner" (19:7). But why would they be scandalized? Jesus' mission on this earth was nothing other than to meet with sinners! "For the Son of Man came to seek out and to save the lost" (19:10). Jesus was not roaming the countryside looking for a few good people to join his cause. He was looking for the only kind of people who can be saved: sinners.

There are a number of biblical understandings, or pictures, of how this saving happens. We might indeed speak of being saved from sin through God's forgiveness. We can also speak of release from bondage through redemption, or of bridging our alienation from God, self, and others through the divine invitation to come home. Perhaps the homecoming theme is most appropriate in Zacchaeus' story, in light of Jesus' words of verse 9: "Salvation has come to this house, because he too is a son of Abraham." Here was a lost son, a man once in the wrong place but now invited back to the right place—the family home where he belonged.

Note that Zacchaeus was not required to "clean up" before accepting the invitation. Naturally, when Jesus calls sinners, an eventual amendment of lifestyle is included. This does not mean that his love is the means and amendment the end. As theologian Anders Nygren puts it: "Love is always an end in itself, and the moment it is degraded into a means to some other end it ceases to be love." How pertinent to our journey of compassion! We extend ourselves in love to all in need, not just because we see the potential in them to be something other than they are but because they are what they are right now: needful. Just as we all are when we come to God.

Third, salvation *requires a readiness to respond.* Anyone who has worked with young children knows the importance of readiness. Before attempting any new skill, children must be ready physically, intellectually, and emotionally. They will need encouragement and guidance from someone who already has mastered those skills.

Helen Keller's experience of learning to communicate is one example of readiness. Her teacher, Ann Sullivan, tried and tried to break through Helen's world of silent darkness. Ann knew she was working with a brilliant mind and a personality waiting to blossom. Ann wanted Helen to realize that the delicate finger movements she repeatedly formed in the little girl's hand were not simply random touches. When arranged together those motions would burst with meaning as letters and words. It was only after she made this connection that Helen was ready to receive the wonderful gift of communication with others.

Likewise, Zacchaeus might not have been ready to receive if Jesus had come to town three weeks earlier. But when he climbed the tree Zacchaeus was ready to see his soon-to-be Lord. What helps us become ready to receive God's salvation? It is the willingness to repent. Karl Menninger, in his book *Whatever Became of Sin?* wrote that we must cry out to our world with a heartfelt message: "Cry comfort, cry repentance, cry hope. Because recognition of our part in the world's transgression is the only remaining hope." Until we are ready to recognize our own sin for what it is, there is little hope of salvation and change.

Fourth, salvation *affects our whole life.* Sometimes we are tempted to view salvation only as a crisis-point of conversion, a rational decision made in one moment in time. When Jesus invited him down from the tree, Zacchaeus experienced an exchange that affected his whole life from that point on. It was more than a change in world view, or a slight cognitive modification. It was as if his heart grew several sizes.

Remember that Zacchaeus had not been doing anything illegal; tax collectors could extract as much money as they wanted under the corrupt Roman system. He certainly was not acting with compassion or justice, however. When salvation came to Zacchaeus' house through Jesus, Zacchaeus did not begin the life of a person we would call "a Sunday Christian." Jesus *entered* his life. A powerful bond was formed that linked Zacchaeus' words and beliefs to his lifestyle. As William Barclay said, "It is not a mere change of words which Jesus Christ demands, but a change of life."

Fifth, salvation *has an impact beyond inner transformation.* We cannot be privately righteous while living with no regard for what is good or bad for our communities and families. Several years ago, a seminary professor was asked by a young woman in a public elevator, "Are you saved?" His response was, "Well, I think so. But to really know, you should ask my wife, my daughter, and my colleagues at school. They are the ones who can tell you if salvation is evident in my life."

The "compassion connection" leaps out in our review of biblical salvation. Zacchaeus was as much the outcast as the sinner. He was alienated from his community, and Jesus called him back into true "sonship" (19:9), inviting him to come home. What was Zacchaeus' response? "I will give to the poor," he said (19:8). How appropriate! Through salvation, our standing with God is indeed changed, but our relationship to God's other children is transformed as well.

Too Easy?

Jesus' message of salvation sounds wonderful, but it can be interpreted in a way that makes it sound almost too simple: just be sorry for what you did and God willingly forgives and forgets. The scriptures remind us, however, that the work of the Savior was neither simple nor easy. A sinless man, Jesus died because of sin in the world. We have the opportunity to know God's love and forgiveness because of that death on the cross, and the resurrection that followed. We are invited to "stand there" (19:8)—at the cross—and repent.

Sometimes I try to make repentance easy. I am sorry for my sin without really wanting to change my ways. Maybe I have been "caught," concerned about the consequences, but hardly determined to change my behavior. After all, perhaps next time I will avoid detection.

Zacchaeus responded swiftly to Jesus' invitation. He welcomed the gentle teacher into his home and volunteered to give half of his possessions to the poor. He would pay back four times any amount he had taken dishonestly. In doing this Zacchaeus went well beyond what the law required for restitution (which called for the original amount plus twenty percent). Thus repentance for Zacchaeus was genuine—the kind that bears fruit. And, no doubt, having gotten salvation, Zacchaeus slept well at night.

Discussion and Action

1. Refer to the first question of the Personal Preparation. Share what salvation means to you. Tell stories about experiences and/or people who helped prepare the way for your salvation. How do you know when you are ready to receive the salvation that Jesus offers?

2. Jesus visited "one who is a sinner" (19:7). Should we understand ourselves as sinners in God's eyes? What does it mean to understand yourself as a sinner—especially in relationship to our society's emphasis on maintaining self-esteem?

3. Zacchaeus was traveling the road of life in the direction of selfishness, but he turned around and determined to follow Jesus in his journey of compassion. How do you think salvation looked to Zacchaeus' wife, children, and colleagues?

4. Why would anyone be inclined to grumble because a sinner accepted salvation? Have you ever felt like grumbling about a situation of renewal?

5. Referring to the relationship between grace and discipline, Richard Foster said in *Celebration of Discipline:* "We do not need to be hung on the horns of the dilemma of either human works or idleness. God has given us the disciplines of the spiritual life as means of receiving his grace. The disciplines allow us to place ourselves before God so that he can transform us." Do you like this way of characterizing

the relationship between grace and discipline? What would you add or clarify?

6. After he received salvation, Zacchaeus immediately began to correct his acts of injustice. What action could your covenant group take this week in response to injustice?

7. Continue to explore a potential sister-church relationship by assessing the interest level in your congregation. Developing a sister-church relationship is a long-term process. Most of the steps so far have involved the gathering of information and assessing interest. If your pastor and a significant number of church members are interested in the idea of a sister-church relationship, assign a person or committee to develop a list of potential churches to contact.

9

What's Left Over?

Luke 20:45—21:4

Speaking of money, nowhere do we find society's values and Kingdom values more in conflict. For most people, the key to life is acquiring more money. But when Jesus spoke on the subject, he left little doubt about what mattered most: having less money left over.

Personal Preparation

1. Read Luke 20:45—21:4. How does this passage touch your life most closely at this time?
2. As you prepare for this session, find a newspaper or magazine article related to the total stewardship of life. Be prepared to share it with your covenant group.
3. Imagine winning the state lottery. What would you do with the money? How would your choices demonstrate your beliefs and priorities?

Understanding

You see them every day on the streets of big cities: the "power dressers." Dark three-piece suits, starched white shirts, striped silk ties, shiny imported leather shoes. Most people would tell you that, in the struggle for success, you start by looking a success.

Who were the power dressers of Jesus' day? He saw them in the marketplaces, the synagogues, and the banquet halls. Rather than three-piece suits, they wore long white linen robes with tassels on the fringe. Only people of leisure and wealth could dress that way. Apparently some of these religious leaders thought they had reached the very pinnacle of prestige—prime candidates for a listing in *Who's*

Who of the First Century. As they walked by the offering boxes, they threw in large coins guaranteed to rattle and clank impressively all the way to the bottom of the box.

Impressive Show . . . or Immense Sacrifice?

Jesus was not impressed. To him the soft "plink-plink" of the widow's two coins was the sound of a sacrificial gift from the heart, the kind of gift that truly meant something despite appearances.

Throughout the Gospel of Luke, Jesus encouraged his disciples to value genuine humility and sacrificial service. In these verses he criticized the practices of some scribes who "devoured" widows' houses while saying long prayers for the sake of appearances. Their actions were inconsistent with the values they professed. On the other hand, the poor widow lived out her values as she quietly contributed two small copper coins at immense sacrifice to her daily budget. In fact, it was "all she had to live on" (21:4).

Jesus apparently assessed the worth of each offering not by how much was given, but by how much was left over. In a society in which widows had no place and no power, religious leaders of that day had to help them manage their property. This was commanded by the law. However, too often these leaders abused their power and took over a widow's property for their own gain. They gave a display of impressive spirituality, but failed to live it.

I cannot be too critical of those religious leaders, however. I often find it quite difficult to keep my lifestyle in line with my professed and sometimes showy values. For any of us today, it can be tough to see the connection between values and lifestyle. We lift up the aerosol can of hair spray or shaving cream in the morning . . . and then stare at the evening news report about the day's air quality. Connection?

Even when we do see the connection, we do not always live up to what we know. In our world today, selfish ambition and greed often contrast with humility and sacrificial giving. This leads to the misuse of power and the evil act of devouring something that should be protected and preserved. A farmer I know wanted to protect his ravine from the trash being dumped into it. He loved God's good creation of earth, air, and water, and he wanted to preserve his little stream and the river it fed. So this man spent an entire day putting up "No Dumping" signs.

The signs lay scattered on the ground the next day. Intruders continued to sneak onto his property at night to leave behind their discarded washers, dryers, refrigerators, and half-filled paint cans. The trespassers were saving themselves some money—while devouring their environment.

Around the world, children are the first to suffer economic oppression and hunger. One ten-year-old girl works long hours in a South Asian carpet factory because of her family's poverty. The factory owner wants to keep wages low, and customers in the West are happy to purchase lovely hand-knotted carpets at bargain prices. Likewise, in the United States, children who need special protection and care are more likely to be living in poverty than any other group of people. Where are the compassionate helpers who know that giving is a sacrificial act of faith in God?

Even in the church we may find it difficult to connect sacrificial giving to our faith. During a time of economic crisis for farmers, a rural Iowa congregation was learning about the stewardship of resources. Someone asked one of the congregational leaders, "Isn't this a poor time to have a stewardship emphasis in the church? Times are so bad right now!" This leader thought seriously about that question, for she knew the horrible impact of the farm crisis on family incomes. She answered: "Is it ever a bad time to emphasize stewardship? For that is what we do as Christians, regardless of our financial circumstances. We are always stewards, either good ones or poor ones. In fact, it may be even more appropriate to emphasize our role as stewards in hard times."

The question is not, How much or how little should I give? Rather it is, How shall I respond to God's blessings in my life? That is the joyous, troublesome question for me, when I remember to ask it. How can I compassionately share with others what I have been given? It is a bittersweet privilege because I know it will require sacrifice, perhaps immense sacrifice. My life is in Christ's hands and I know that until his values become second nature for me—as my daily lifestyle—I cannot be truly compassionate.

Insidious Suggestions . . . or Intimate Service?

Sacrifice is tough in uncertain economic times, but we face another formidable hurdle in living out our professed values. It is the insidious suggestions bombarding us in the media. The seductive message of our media culture is that spiritual fulfillment can come through physical attainment. Lecturer and writer Tony Campolo, in *Wake up America,* eloquently sums up the challenge:

In our TV ads, it is as though the ecstasy of the spirit experienced by a St. Theresa or a St. Francis can be reduced to the gratification coming from a particular car. And the kind of love that Christ compared to His love for the church can be expressed by buying the right kind of wristwatch for that special person in your life. . . . Hitherto, spiritual gratification could come only via spiritual means. Thus, people were urged to choose between the things of this world and the blessings of God. Now, that duality has been overcome. Ours is an age in which spiritual blessings are being promised to those who buy material things. The spiritual is being absorbed by the physical. The fruit of the spirit, suggests the media, can be had without God.

Carol June Hooker refuses to listen to that suggestion. She practices community health nursing at the infirmary of a large homeless shelter in Washington, D.C. Her patients have many serious problems: drug or alcohol addiction, mental illness, violent behavior, infectious diseases such as AIDS and tuberculosis. These patients need immediate, drastic health care measures. Nevertheless, the first treatment they receive upon arrival is to have their feet washed in a pail of warm water. As Carol and her staff gently massage dirty, blistered, smelly, cracked feet with their hands, the patients seem to relax. They become temporarily more lucid and less violent. They are able to connect with another human being who has willingly humbled herself to serve them.

Compassion that grows out of humility and a spirit of service is beautiful to behold even when it involves kneeling and washing ugly feet. We do not have to succumb to the suggestion that the "good life" requires gathering more possessions or dressing in the latest fashions. Instead, great goodness rises up out of every ordinary act of human compassion.

Discussion and Action

1. Share the newspaper or magazine articles you found during personal preparation. In light of Luke 20:45—21:4, how do you think Jesus might apply the concept of the total stewardship of life to these contemporary situations?

2. Focus on Personal Preparation question 3 for a few minutes. What would you do with your new lottery fortunes? What role would wise stewardship play for you?

3. What is one way your lifestyle choices might become more in line with your values during the next month?

4. Tithing is a response of gratitude for God's gifts. Under the Jewish law, tithing was required (Lev. 27:30). Does Jesus' call to humility and service require us to tithe?

5. How would you have answered the Iowa farmer's question about stewardship?

6. In contrast to the scribes, the poor widow contributed all she had to the treasury. In other words, she was able to trust fully in God for what she needed. While we may not advocate giving everything away, it is important to raise the question, What does total trust in God mean for me? How do you respond?

7. Brainstorm for a few minutes about this question: What can our church do to show people how to begin creative forms of stewardship? Here are two suggestions: consider offering workshops on money management to young couples, or have a young people's teach-in on recycling. Do you have other ideas? If you are moving toward a potential sister-church relationship, consider what financial resources you could use in contributing to another congregation's needs.

8. Brainstorm further steps you need to take related to the sister-church partnership. Ideally, your initial work during these early weeks will culminate in a presentation to your Witness Commission and/or Church Board for consideration by the entire congregation. Those experienced in sister-church ministry stress the need for a strong vote of congregational approval—at least two-thirds or more.

10

Compassion Multiplied
Luke 22:39-46

In an agonizing night of prayer, Jesus asked that the cross be removed from his future. He struggled with the will of God, ultimately choosing the way of compassion motivated by obedience. Our own compassion grows as we learn more about God's true nature and respond in obedience. Christ's love is multiplied as we learn to embody his compassion in our world.

Personal Preparation

1. Read through Luke 22:39-46. Reflect on Jesus' anguish in the garden. When have you wrestled with the will of God? How did God respond?
2. Think about times you have risked new experiences in a different culture. How did this affect your faith perspective?
3. Take to your group meeting a picture, plaque, or sculpture that reminds you of Jesus praying in the garden. What is the meaning of this picture for you?

Understanding

I was just fifteen years old, traveling with thirty other teenagers on a mission trip to Jamaica, Haiti, and Puerto Rico. We all lived and worked closely with each other, but during our free time we tended to gravitate to kids we knew well. On our first night at a new work site, the final weekend of the trip, we gathered just before bedtime to receive new room assignments. My roommate for the next few days would be the only African American girl in our group. I was the only Southerner, having grown up in Mississippi. Being assigned a black roommate was not a startling experience for me, but it was certainly a surprise.

Rhonda and I gathered our luggage and went off together to find our room. We wasted little time getting ready for bed because we were exhausted. However, I was feeling unsure and a bit nervous in this new situation. After we said our goodnights, I could hardly wait to scoot down into the security and warmth of my sleeping bag. As I was readying my "nest" for a night of much needed rest, I noticed the picture hanging above my bed—the familiar picture of Jesus praying in the garden. As I looked more closely, I saw that Jesus, in this particular rendition of the scene, was black.

He Was Obedient

It may seem like a little thing, but that picture set off an internal earthquake. It challenged me to take off inner blinders that had kept my world safe and predictable. I grew up in a neighborhood in which African Americans were considered second-class citizens. My compassion had been limited; I needed to strip away a layer of prejudice.

There is a direct connection between the quality of relationship with God and the ability to reach out to God's people. We have been saying this in different ways throughout this study. In this instance, the "quality" was affected by my changing perceptions of the wideness of God's mercy. I grew up in a time and a place that narrowed my vision of Jesus, but I did not give my upbringing much thought until Rhonda became the focus of a potential friendship. Now I was faced with a call to obedience and compassion. So was Rhonda.

Our compassion for others grows as we respond obediently to God's leading in our lives. Even for Jesus, obedience was the foundation of compassion. When he trudged up the Mount of Olives to pray, his prayer was "not my will but yours be done" (22:42). As he approached the ultimate act of compassion, of giving up his life for others, he agonized over God's will until his sweat became like great drops of blood.

As children, obedience is one of the words we learn to dislike. As adults, most of us have not changed our attitudes about obedience. To obey means to surrender, to submit to the control of another. We prefer to be in control of our own lives, like a toddler who insists, "I'll do it myself." Perhaps that yearning to be in control is what prompted a friend of mine to reveal her difficulty in singing the words of the hymn "Trust and Obey." Do you have trouble with that hymn? To obey is to humble ourselves more than we would like. We may even resist kneeling in prayer because that very act puts us too far down, too close to the floor, to be in control. Luke presents Jesus as a model of submission to God's will. On that night of prayer, Jesus, in all his human anxiety about the pain awaiting him, chose to obey. We must not take lightly what that night meant for him, for the same struggle is our own heritage today as we live out the life of Jesus in us.

We Are the Embodiment

Our hope as Christians is this: the compassion of Jesus did not stop with the anguish of the garden or the agony of the cross. If we are the body of Christ in the world today, then we take up his work of active compassion now that he is no longer physically on earth to do it himself. The early church father Augustine wrote:

> What does love look like?
> It has the hands to help others.
> It has the feet to hasten to the poor and needy.
> It has the eyes to see misery and want.
> It has the ears to hear sighs and sorrows.
> That is what love looks like.

We are the embodiment of Christ's ongoing compassion. In *The Alleluia Affair* by Malcolm Boyd, compassion is multiplied throughout the world as figures of Jesus come down from crosses everywhere in order to embrace people in need. One Jesus figure, who escaped from a stained-glass window in a large church, joined migrant farm workers. Other figures entered into the mundane places of life, meeting ordinary people. Here was Jesus at a city lunch counter, breaking bread in the form of a hamburger bun and drinking coffee with other customers. Jesus—working in a bus terminal, or in a restaurant, or with a construction crew. As people encountered the physical embodiment of compassion in their daily lives, their understandings of God's love took on new meaning.

When we are obedient to God's call, we too begin to embody compassion. When we see the reality of Jesus' presence in others' lives, our hands and feet are moved to reach out. Patricia Tucker Spier, following a trip to southern Africa, told how this principle was played out in the common life of a mission church. She spoke of a train station and a nearby construction site in downtown Johannesburg. There many homeless men congregated each day, having come from countries all over central and southern Africa in search of work. They wanted to work down in the mines, hoping to earn enough money to send a bit home to their hungry families.

Missionary Diane Wicks had begun a homeless ministry in the nearby church, offering the men a Sunday evening worship service. During the announcement time Diane held a mail call, giving out letters from home that were addressed to the church. Her church was a place of worship but also a place where the "unknown" homeless could be known and found.

Patricia worshiped with this compassionate missionary and at the end of one service was asked to help serve Communion. She recalled the men coming to the front of the church, kneeling to receive the bread and cup. Several of them had been injured—perhaps in fights or muggings—and they wore dirty bandages. One man, with a huge gash in his forehead, leaned on the Communion rail wearing a shirt splashed with dried blood.

"I bent over," said Patricia, "bowing to serve each kneeling man the bread of the Eucharist with the words: 'The body of Christ, broken for you.' Where there was a forehead covered with a dirty bandage, there could have been a crown of thorns. And I wondered if anyone would ever cast lots for *this* bloodstained shirt. Who was I to proclaim to one so broken, 'The body of Christ, broken for you?' Yet, according to the Gospel, good news of all good news, the divine brokenness somehow redeems our human one."

After all ate and partook from a common cup, the two women offered one another the elements. "Diane offered me the cup. And in one of those flashes of thought that pass through our minds, I realized that this was, indeed, a *common* cup. The men—homeless, sick, injured—had all touched their lips to this same chalice. And now it was being offered to me. 'The blood of Christ, poured out for you.' For me, and you. And them. Will we drink? I don't know if I hesitated outwardly; perhaps it was only a hesitation of spirit. But it felt like a defining moment."

Will you and I drink from the cup, as Patricia did?

As Jesus did?

Naturally, we too will dare to pray: "Remove this cup from me!" (22:42) But will we drink nevertheless? When we are obedient to God's call we begin to embody compassion. It is, on many levels, a life-endangering call. "Compassion is the sometimes fatal capacity for feeling what it's like to live inside somebody else's skin," said Frederick Buechner. "It is the knowledge that there can never really be any peace and joy for me until there is peace and joy finally for you too."

Discussion and Action

1. Begin by focusing on the opening story of this session. In what ways can you relate to it? When have you experienced a similar situation in your life? When has Jesus been revealed in a different light?

2. Refer to Personal Preparation question 3. Share the picture, plaque, or sculpture that reminds you of Jesus praying in the garden. Talk about the meaning this picture has for you. Ask how the humanity of Jesus, who struggled with God's will, is a comfort to you. In what ways is his obedience a challenge for you to emulate?

3. When have you wanted to discover or clarify God's will during an especially difficult time? How much insight did you receive in advance? In hindsight?

4. What does it mean for you, in practical terms, to be Jesus' hands, feet, eyes, and ears in the world? What might it mean for your group? In what ways can this calling be a great joy? How is it a significant burden?

5. Writer-priest Louis Evely said, "Inside of every human being God exists and waits to be detected so that He may thrive." What is your response to this statement? How does the statement relate to Patricia's story? How does it relate to people you have met in your lifetime?

6. Consider closing your ten weeks together by sharing in bread and cup Communion. Use the words, "This is the body of Christ, broken for you; this is the blood of Christ, poured out for you." Consider passing a common cup around the circle, with the option of intinction.

Suggestions for Sharing and Prayer

This material is designed for covenant groups that spend one hour sharing and praying together, followed by one hour of Bible study. The suggestions given here may help relate the group's sharing and praying time to the study of *A Spirituality of Compassion*. You will find session-by-session ideas followed by general resources. Use those you find most helpful, and bring your own creative ideas to your group.

1. You Can't Force the Heart

❑ Take time to get acquainted. Some of you may have been together in a group in the past, but remember that now you will become a unique and special group because of a new study focus and new members. Take a few minutes to begin learning about each other: (1) state your name, (2) tell the group about an early memory of someone you consider to be compassionate, and (3) identify a compassionate person today.

❑ Focus on the theme of "forcing the heart." Ask for volunteers to talk about times they have tried to make themselves do something they did not want to do. You might limit the sharing to memories from childhood, for example, a memory of trying to eat spinach or asparagus because parents said, "It's good for you!" Encourage some humor in this reflection. Is it possible to like a food through sheer willpower? Is it possible to become more compassionate through willpower?

❑ The authors of this study say that "when confronted with difficult truths about themselves, people do tend to become angry." Invite married people in the group to tell—with permission from their spouses—about harmless but irritating habits of the other. Follow this lighthearted sharing by talking about times you have recognized your own anger as indicating a more serious relational flaw.

❑ Ask everyone who has pocket change to take out a coin. Remind members of the group that throughout this ten-week study you will be challenged to think about *compassion* and *prayer* as two sides of the same coin—not heads or tails but "hearts" or "feet." We cannot have one without the other. After a few moments of silent reflection, invite people to say whether they sense more need for the "heart" (a deeper devotional life) or the "feet" (greater compassionate, active involvement) in their lives. Break into two groups for prayer—the "hearts" and the "feet." Pray for yourselves, the members of your small group, and those in the other group. Come back together as a whole group and briefly share insights from discussion or concerns raised in the smaller groups.

❑ As a group, complete this sentence: "Prayer is. . . ." Make a list of possible sentences and keep it handy for use in future sessions. Ask everyone to continue to think about the nature of prayer in their times of personal preparation. Consider adding new sentences to the list each time you meet.

❑ Share prayer concerns by inviting each person in the group to tell about people or situations for which prayer is needed. As each person shares, the group response may be, "Hear our prayer, O Lord." You each may identify one particular concern and tell the group what you plan to do about it this week. *Agree to pray for one another in the coming week.*

❑ Close by singing or reading in unison, the words of the hymn "Lord, speak to me," "Will You Let Me Be Your Servant?" or another hymn of service. First, listen as one person reads each verse aloud, then sing that verse after contemplating the words.

2. Being and Doing . . . in Balance

❑ Last week you agreed to pray for one another as you took action. Share with each other about your times of prayer and action. Tell the group how you will continue in action for your prayer concern in the week to come, or identify a new concern for which you plan to take action.

❑ Focus on the session theme of balance. Imagine that your group is on a giant seesaw. How would you divide up half on one side of the room and half on the other side—in order to make the seesaw perfectly balanced?

Have some fun splitting up for balance, but follow this rule: all of your moves should be made in silence until the group seems to be balanced. Then, anonymously on slips of paper, write down your weight. Shuffle the slips in the two separate group piles— one on one side of the room and one on the other. Have someone total the weight for each side. How close did you come to balancing? Now talk about how you personally or as a group try to balance activity with time alone with God.

❏ Eric Fromm said, "We have developed a phobia of being alone." When have you been phobic in that way? What did you do?

❏ What are you like when you have nothing planned? Is it easy or hard for you to just be? Relate your responses to how you plan— or do not plan—your vacations.

❏ What is the most dangerous thing that you have done because of your faith in Christ? What is your mission in life? How do your daily activities move you to fulfill your mission?

❏ Close by singing the hymn "Take Time to Be Holy." Especially note the words, which show the balance between the spiritual life and compassionate response.

3. A 'Doing' that Risks

❏ Share about your prayer and/or action during the past week. Identify your concern for prayer and action for the week to come.

❏ Have you ever been thrust into a situation of potential ministry but felt not-yet-ready? What did you do? How would you describe the different roles of training and dependence on God's Spirit when it comes to reaching out?

❏ The disciples were caught off guard by a sudden, awesome revelation in the midst of ordinary life. In light of this story, respond to the following statement by Thomas Moore, in *The Care of Souls:* "Spirituality is seeded, germinates, sprouts, and blossoms in the mundane. It is to be found and nurtured in the smallest of daily activities. The spirituality that feeds the soul and ultimately heals our psychological wounds may be found in those sacred objects that dress themselves in the accoutrements of the ordinary." Talk about times you have experienced the sacred in the ordinary.

❏ The authors of this study stress the value of opening up to one another. Assess the climate of your group in this regard. On a chalkboard or poster board, draw up a scale similar to the one below to represent the climate in your group. As group members offer comments, work on coming to a consensus about what number would characterize your group.

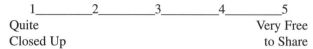

1_____2_____3_____4_____5
Quite   Very Free
Closed Up   to Share

Then discuss what it would take for your group to move a step closer to number 5.

❑ Spend some time in silence as a way to encounter God. Ask everyone to "be present to God's presence" for a few minutes. Let the group know that after seven minutes of silence a signal will be given, perhaps the ringing of a small bell or knocking on a table. This will remind people to push aside their distracting thoughts gently and come back to awareness of God's presence. After three more minutes, a group member may begin singing softly, "Spirit of the Living God." Everyone may join in to close your time of contemplative prayer.

4. The Fear Is Real

❑ Share your prayers and actions of this last week. What acts of compassion do you hope to live out in the week to come?

❑ Respond to this quotation by Aleksandr Solzhenitsyn, in *The First Circle:* "There was peace in their hearts. They were filled with the fearlessness of those who have lost *everything,* the fearlessness which is not easy to come by, but which endures." Have you ever experienced the courage of "all-is-lost"? How does this courage relate to trusting God in a time of crisis or persecution?

❑ Share joys and concerns. Have construction paper and crayons available. Draw or make a mask to hide something that you would prefer others not know about you. If you are willing, share about these things with your group. It is alright simply to signify your fear with a mask. Ask for prayers regarding these "silent requests." Close this time by reading in unison the hymn "Healer of our every ill" or "There is a balm."

❑ As a unison confession, pray together Psalm 130, each one reading from a preferred translation.

❑ The authors of this study mention harmful secrets. Think about any such secrets in your own lives. During a period of silence, gather in a circle and turn to the person on your right. Lay hands gently on his or her shoulders as one group member offers prayer for healing inner hurts or slowly reads the words of Psalm 121 as a benediction.

5. Definitely Unconventional

❑ Talk about your prayers and actions of the past week. Share plans for prayer and action for the coming week.

❑ Talk about people you have known and admired, who have suffered courageously with a long-lasting physical ailment. How would you compare this type of courage to the kinds we often hear about in the media, sports, politics, or the military?

❑ When our spiritual lives and our compassionate actions are out of balance with each other, we are in a sense "bent over," not free to live in God's grace. When have you been "bent over"? What binds you today?

❑ William Walsh wrote, "I can endure my own despair but not another's hope." Have you ever secretly been upset or jealous at someone else's good fortune? How do you handle that kind of feeling?

❑ The religious leaders in Luke 13 reacted poorly to the unconventional. Make a list of things that would fall into the category of "the way we've always done it" in your congregation. Review your list and consider alternative ways of doing these things that might be suggested by a new believer, a new church member, or a teenager. How upsetting would these new ideas be for your church? What would happen if some of the ideas were welcomed?

❑ In a church drama enacted by teenagers, the healed woman of Luke 13 does cartwheels down the aisle. When your life has been touched with great joy, as was the woman's, what does your response of praise look like? What do you do? Share some responses of joy that you have offered to God, or would like to offer right now.

❑ Name favorite scriptures of joy and praise, then select one or two group members to read some of these scripture passages aloud as your benediction.

6. It Costs *What?*

❑ Check in with each other regarding your prayers and actions from last week. Share your prayer and action plans for the coming week.

❑ In Luke 14:34-35, Jesus talked about disciples who lost their initial enthusiasm for the faith. Have there been times when your commitment to Jesus waned? What was that like? Were you able to regain your commitment? How?

❑ Use chalkboard and chalk, or newsprint and markers, to draw a two-column chart. Together compare salvation by grace to the costly call to discipleship. Jot down comments and responses in the appropriate columns. As you view the chart, talk about how you demonstrate the distinction in day-to-day living.

❑ Look at the words of the hymn "Count Well the Cost." How would these words have spoken to the founders of your particular denomination? How do they touch your life or your journey of compassion today?

"Count well the cost," Christ Jesus says, "when you lay the foundation."
Are you resolved, though all seem lost, to risk your reputation,
Yourself, your wealth, for Christ the Lord
As you now give your solemn word?

❑ Ask for volunteers to share the hymns they chose for Personal Preparation question 3. Talk about the meaning these hymns have for your confession of faith and your journey of compassion. Sing some of the hymns as prayers of praise, petition, and intercession.

7. Keep on Knocking

❑ During a check-in time, ask each other to talk about "where you are" at the moment:
  •a feeling to share?
  •a report of success or progress?
  •a problem or struggle to tell about?

•a troubling question to raise?

•an insight to convey?

Then share your prayer and action plans for the coming week.

❑ Look for prayer hymns in your hymnal. How many of these talk about being persistent in prayer, even when answers do not seem to come?

❑ Have there been times when God seemed far away and distant? Tell the group about those times.

❑ Read Hebrews 11:29-40, focusing especially on verse 39. How would you respond to a critic of Christianity who said, "See, God never came through for these people of faith. You should not expect it either"?

❑ Sometimes people say, "Thank God that I did not get what I was praying for at the time!" Have you ever said that? What have you learned from such experiences?

❑ Ask everyone in your group to spend a moment in silence, thinking about personal or general prayer requests that have gone unanswered. With eyes closed, take turns naming those requests. After each comment, the group may offer this prayer refrain: "O Lord, how long shall I cry for help, and you will not listen?" (Hab. 1:2)

8. Welcome, Lord!

❑ Check in with each other about your prayer concerns and resulting actions. Each of you may tell the group your plans for next week.

❑ Share a favorite Bible text about salvation. Why has this text been meaningful to you?

❑ Talk about the different ways Jesus presents the idea of salvation in the Gospels. What stories and metaphors speak most powerfully to you?

❑ The authors point out that salvation cannot be a purely private transaction. Beyond inner transformation, salvation must issue in acts of compassion. How does your own salvation experience motivate you to reach out to others? Or, in light of Philippians 2:12-13, how is salvation working itself out in your life these days? Can you share an example?

❑ Each person may select a hymn of salvation. Sing some or all of the selections.

9. What's Left Over?

❑ Share how your prayer concerns and actions are going. Have these experiences moved you to more balance between your prayer life and compassionate action? How? Tell the group about your plans for next week.

❑ Offer this prayer of confession in unison, inviting all to kneel:

Hold our requests in abeyance, Lord,
Until we are willing to serve instead of be served;
Until we are more concerned for justice than our comfort;
Until we walk the second mile without complaint;
Until we sacrifice so others may eat;
Until we right our wronged relationships;
Until we do our part to build the church for which Christ died.

We often run from the demands of the Gospel
While expecting our demands to be met.
Forgive our cowardice and neglect.
We repent of our posturing and pettiness.
Energize our discipleship that we may serve Thee
In the need of others, for Thy Kingdom's sake. Amen.

From *Prayers for Worship*, by E. Lee Phillips. Baker Book House, 1985. Used by permission.

❑ Does your church have an unofficial dress code? How would you describe it?

❑ What is your definition of living a simple life? Consider these questions: Is it okay for a Christian to have nice things? Is there such a thing as pride in being poor—or being poorer than someone else?

❑ Look at hymns about the act of giving out of joyous response to what God has given us. When has giving been a chore for you? When has it been a joyful response of gratitude?

❑ Following Jesus' example, gently but thoroughly wash one another's feet (or hands), using a basin or pail and large towels. Silently pray for the person whose feet you wash. In what ways does this action remind you of the widow's gift?

❏ Close with the Prayer Following Footwashing (in the General Resources section).

10. Compassion Multiplied

❏ If you are willing, share your experiences of wrestling with the will of God. How do you characterize those experiences as you look back on them? What aspects of growth did they bring to your life?

❏ Luke 22:39-42 speaks to us of God's deep passion, of God's "feeling with" people. Talk about what this means. Is it a comforting thought during tough times?

❏ Sing together hymns of Jesus' passion, such as, "'Tis Midnight and on Olive's Brow."

❏ Take out your wallets and remove each item that identifies you, such as driver's licenses, credit cards, club memberships, etc. Show a picture or two to others, and note how you have changed over the years.

Then think back over your experiences during this ten-week study, in which you have worked to balance your growing spiritual awareness with a growing ability to reach out. How has your identity changed during this time? How are you different, and how are you the same?

❏ In pairs or small groups, make a covenant together for the coming weeks. Do you plan to continue your disciplines of prayer and action? In what ways?

❏ For your closing, pray or sing together the hymn, "In the Bulb There Is a Flower."

General Sharing and Prayer Resources

Forming a Covenant Group

Covenant Expectations

Covenant-making is significant throughout the biblical story. God made covenants with Noah, Abraham, and Moses. Jeremiah speaks about God making a covenant with the people, "written on the heart." In the New Testament, Jesus is identified as the mediator of the new covenant, and the early believers lived out of covenant relationships. Throughout history people have lived in covenant relationship with God and within community.

Christians today also covenant with God and make commitments to each other. Such covenants help believers live out their faith. God's empowerment comes to them as they gather in covenant community to pray and study, share and receive, reflect and act.

People of the Covenant is a program that is anchored in this covenantal history of God's people. It is a network of covenantal relationships. Denominations, districts or regions, congregations, small groups, and individuals all make covenants. Covenant group members commit themselves to the mission statement, seeking to become more:

—biblically informed so that they better understand the revelation of God;

—globally aware so that they know themselves to be better connected with all of God's world; and

—relationally sensitive to God, self, and others.

The Burlap Cross Symbol
The imperfections of the burlap cross, its rough texture and unrefined fabric, the interweaving of threads, the uniqueness of each strand, are elements present in the covenant group. The people in the groups are imperfect, unpolished, interrelated with each other, yet still unique beings.

The shape that this collection of imperfect threads creates is the cross, symbolizing for all Christians the resurrection and presence of Christ our Savior. A covenant group is something akin to this burlap cross. It unites common, ordinary people and sends them out again in all directions to be in the world.

Prayer of Praise for a Compassionate God

Praise the One who hears the cry of the poor,
  who lifts up the weak and gives them strength.
Praise the One who feeds the hungry
  and satisfies the longing of those in need.
Praise the One who holds with tenderness the orphan and widow
  and gives the stranger a land and a home.

Isaiah 61:1-2 NRSV. Adapted in *Hymnal: A Worship Book,* 1992.

Prayers of Compassion

God our healer,
   whose mercy is like a refining fire,
touch us with your judgment,
   and confront us with your tenderness;
   that, being comforted by you,
   we may reach out to a troubled world,
   through Jesus Christ. AMEN.

Reprinted from *All Desires Known* by Janet Morley. Copyright 1988 Morehouse Publishing. Used by permission.

Gracious God,
we thank you for gifts that belong not to us alone,
   but to all our sisters and brothers,
   since they, too, are created in your image.
Let their need become our need;
   let their hunger become our hunger;
   and grant to us also a portion of their pain,
   so that in sharing ourselves,
   we discover the Christ who walks
   with our brothers and sisters. AMEN.

By Kenneth I. Morse in *We Gather Together.* Copyright 1979 Brethren Press.

Benediction

Gentle God,
   you have come near to us
   and have shown us your patience,
   compassion, and love.
As we go, O God,
   give us patience when people are indifferent to your Word,
   give us compassion for the needs of the world,
   and give us love which reflects your forgiveness and grace,
   through Jesus Christ, our Savior. AMEN.

Reprinted from *Hymnal: A Worship Book.* Copyright 1992 The Hymnal Project.

Devotional Readings for This Study

Psalm 130
Psalm 103:1-18
Habakkuk 1:1-2 and 2:2-3
John 13:1-17

Praying Through Action

While marching in Selma, Alabama, for civil rights, Rabbi Abraham Heschel was overheard to say, "I feel like my feet are praying." In recalling the rabbi's statement in the book *Praying for Friends and Enemies,* author Jane E. Vennard explains, "Our hands pray when we help to build a house for Habitat for Humanity. Our eyes pray when we read to the blind. Our ears pray when we listen with compassion to the struggles of another. Our arms pray when we embrace and hold a grieving friend."

From the March 1996 *Agenda,* a publication of the Church of the Brethren General Board Office of Interpretation.

Names and addresses of opportunities and organizations that invite compassionate prayers of service and action:

Church World Service/CROP
P.O. Box 968
Elkhart, IN 46515

Habitat for Humanity
121 Habitat St.
Americus, GA 31709

Heifer Project International
P.O. Box 808
Little Rock, AR 72203

Denominational projects such as Volunteer Disaster Response, workcamps, and other volunteer service projects

Community food pantries and homeless shelters.

Develop a Sister-Church Relationship

Enter into a partnership with another congregation. Develop this relationship with a church in another country or of another ethnic or socioeconomic makeup. Share mutual compassion through prayers for each other, mutual sharing of needs, spiritual gifts, and other resources. To find a church with whom you can partner, contact your denominational headquarters, regional or district ministers, or talk with congregations in your community ecumenical association. For example, one person to contact for information about forming a sister-church relationship is:

Terry Shumaker
"Compañeros en Ministerio"
4504 W. 300 N.
Decatur, IN 46733
(219) 565-3797
Fax (219) 565-3757

"Get acquainted" approaches sister-churches have used:
Have telephone interviews and conference calls by speakerphone between pastors and/or committee members. Record the interview for playing later to the Church Board, Sunday school, or fellowship groups, or loan the tape to individuals.

Exchange videotapes of church activities, along with church photo directories. Exchange newsletters and/or bulletins. Read lists of joys and concerns in each congregation on Sunday mornings or at other gatherings. Exchange lists of people wanting to be pen pals or prayer partners. Exchange recipes by women or men of the two churches.

Other mutual ministry ideas for sister-churches
Offer training seminars and workshops given by the respective congregations, exchanging ministry teams and leaders. Host families from the partner church for a particular work or ministry sharing. Host relocating families for one week while these people explore the area and the employment potential. Exchange music ministry teams. Share any particular ministry as a gift to the other congregation. Worship together, or do pulpit exchanges. Praise together through the exchange of soloists, choirs, bands, and worship teams. Exchange teaching and witness teams. Get involved in workcamp experiences at each of the two churches or church communities, or at a mission site. Do short-term member visits.

Litany for Footwashing

Leader: O Eternal Wisdom, O Vulnerable God,
                 we praise you and give you thanks,
                         because you laid aside your power as a garment
                         and took upon you the form of a slave.

People: You became obedient unto death,
even death on a cross,
receiving authority and comfort
from the hands of a woman;
for God chose what is weak in the world
to shame the strong,
and God chose what is low and despised in the world,
to bring to nothing things that are.

ALL: *Therefore, with the woman who gave you birth,*
the women who befriended you and fed you,
the woman who anointed you for death,
the women who met you, risen from the dead,
we praise you.

Leader: Blessed is our brother Jesus,
who on this night, before Passover,
rose from supper, laid aside his garments,
took a towel and poured water,
and washed his disciples' feet, saying to them:
"If I, your Lord and Teacher,
have washed your feet,
you also ought to wash one another's feet.
If you know these things,
blessed are you if you do them.
If I do not wash you,
you have no part in me."

People: Lord, not my feet only
but also my hands and my head.

ALL: *Come now, tender Spirit of our God,*
wash us and make us one body in Christ;
that, as we are bound together
in this gesture of love,
we may no longer be in bondage
to the principalities and powers
that enslave creation,
but may know your liberating peace
such as the world cannot give. AMEN.

Prayer Following Footwashing

Lord Jesus,
>   we have knelt before each other
>   as you once knelt before your disciples,
>   washing one another's feet.
> We have done what words stammer to express.
> Accept this gesture of love as a pledge
>   of how we mean to live our lives.
> Bless us, as you promised,
>   with joy and perseverance in the way of the cross. AMEN.

By John D. Rempel. Copyright 1991. Used by permission.

A Reading on Compassion

No one can help anyone without becoming involved, without entering with his [or her] whole person into the painful situation, without taking the risk of becoming hurt, wounded, or even destroyed in the process. The beginning and end of all Christian leadership is to give your life for others. Thinking about martyrdom can be an escape unless we realize that real martyrdom means a witness that starts with the willingness to cry with those who cry, laugh with those who laugh, and to make one's own painful and joyful experiences available as sources of clarification and understanding.

Who can save a child from a burning house without taking the risk of being hurt by the flames? Who can listen to a story of loneliness and despair without taking the risk of experiencing similar pains in his own heart and even losing his precious peace of mind? In short: "Who can take away suffering without entering it?"

By Henri J. M. Nouwen, *The Wounded Healer,* copyright 1979.

Living for Jesus

1 Liv-ing for Je-sus a life that is true, Striv-ing to please Him in
2 Liv-ing for Je-sus who died in my place, Bear-ing on Cal-v'ry my
3 Liv-ing for Je-sus thru earth's lit-tle while, My dear-est treas-ure the

all that I do, Yield-ing al - le-giance, glad - heart-ed and free –
sin and dis - grace – Such love con - strains me to an-swer His call,
light of His smile, Seek-ing the lost ones He died to re - deem,

Chorus

This is the path-way of bles-ing for me.
Fol - low His lead - ing and give Him my all. O Je-sus, Lord and
Bring-ing the wea - ry to find rest in Him.

Sav-ior, I give my-self to Thee, For Thou in Thine a - tone-ment didst

Text: Thomas O. Chisholm, 1866-1960
Music: C. Harold Lowden, 1883-1963

give Thy - self for　me. I　own no oth - er　Mas - ter – my heart shall be Thy

throne: My　life I give, hence - forth to live, O　Christ, for Thee a - lone.

In the bulb there is a flower

1 In the bulb there is a flow - er; in the seed, an ap - ple tree;
2 There's a song in ev - 'ry si - lence, seek-ing word and mel - o - dy.
3 In our end is our be - gin - ning; in our time, in - fin - i - ty;

in co - coons, a hid - den prom - ise: but - ter - flies will soon be free!
There's a dawn in ev - 'ry dark - ness, bring-ing hope to you and me.
in our doubt there is be - liev - ing; in our life, e - ter - ni - ty.

In the cold and snow of win - ter there's a spring that waits to be,
From the past will come the fu - ture; what it holds, a mys - ter - y,
In our death, a res - ur - rec - tion; at the last, a vic - to - ry,

un - re - vealed un - til its sea - son, some-thing God a - lone can see.

Text and music: Natalie Sleeth
Copyright 1986 by Hope Publishing Co., Carol Stream, IL 60188

Take time to be holy

1 Take time to be ho - ly, Speak oft with thy Lord;
2 Take time to be ho - ly, The world rush - es on;
3 Take time to be ho - ly, Let Him be thy Guide,
4 Take time to be ho - ly, Be calm in thy soul,

A - bide in Him al - ways, And feed on His Word;
Spend much time in se - cret With Je - sus a - lone;
And run not be - fore Him, What - ev - er be - tide;
Each thought and each mo - tive Be - neath His con - trol;

Make friends of God's chil - dren, Help those who are weak,
By look - ing to Je - sus, Like Him thou shalt be;
In joy or in sor - row, Still fol - low thy Lord,
Thus led by His Spir - it To foun - tains of love,

For - get - ting in noth - ing His bless - ing to seek.
Thy friends in thy con - duct His like - ness shall see.
And, look - ing to Je - sus, Still trust in His Word.
Thou soon shalt be fit - ted For ser - vice, a - bove.

Text: W. D. Longstaff, 1822-1894
Music: George C. Stebbins, 1846-1945